How to
Creatively Finance
Your Real Estate Investments And
Build Your Personal Fortune

What Smart Investors Need To Know—Explained Simply

By
Susan Smith Alvis

How To Creatively Finance Your Real Estate Investments And Build Your Personal Fortune: What Smart Investors Need To Know—Explained Simply

Copyright © 2007 Atlantic Publishing Group, Inc.
1405 SW 6th Avenue • Ocala, Florida 34474 • Phone 800-814-1132 • Fax 352-622-5836
Web site: www.atlantic-pub.com • E-mail: sales@atlantic-pub.com
SAN Number: 268-1250

ISBN 10: 0-910627-04-5   ISBN 13: 978-0-910627-04-7

Library of Congress Cataloging-in-Publication Data

Alvis, Susan Smith, 1969-
   How to creatively finance your real estate investments and build your personal fortune: what smart investors need to know explained simply / Author: Susan Smith Alvis.
        p. cm.
   Includes bibliographical references and index.
   ISBN 10: 0-910627-04-5 (alk. paper)
   ISBN 13: 978-0-910627-04-7 (alk. paper)
   1. Real estate investment--Finance. I. Title.

   HD1382.5.A483 2007
   332.63'24--dc22
                                    2006035620

EDITORIAL CREDIT: Marie Lujanac • mlujanac817@yahoo.com
PROOFREADER: Angela C. Adams • angela.c.adams@hotmail.com
ART DIRECTION & FRONT COVER: Meg Buchner • megadesn@mchsi.com

Printed on Recycled Paper

Printed in the United States

We recently lost our beloved pet "Bear," who was not only our best and dearest friend but also the "Vice President of Sunshine" here at Atlantic Publishing. He did not receive a salary but worked tirelessly 24 hours a day to please his parents. Bear was a rescue dog that turned around and showered myself, my wife Sherri, his grandparents Jean, Bob and Nancy and every person and animal he met (maybe not rabbits) with friendship and love. He made a lot of people smile every day.

We wanted you to know that a portion of the profits of this book will be donated to The Humane Society of the United States.

–Douglas & Sherri Brown

THE HUMANE SOCIETY
OF THE UNITED STATES ©

The human-animal bond is as old as human history. We cherish our animal companions for their unconditional affection and acceptance. We feel a thrill when we glimpse wild creatures in their natural habitat or in our own backyard.

Unfortunately, the human-animal bond has at times been weakened. Humans have exploited some animal species to the point of extinction.

The Humane Society of the United States makes a difference in the lives of animals here at home and worldwide. The HSUS is dedicated to creating a world where our relationship with animals is guided by compassion. We seek a truly humane society in which animals are respected for their intrinsic value, and where the human-animal bond is strong.

Want to help animals? We have plenty of suggestions. Adopt a pet from a local shelter, join The Humane Society and be a part of our work to help companion animals and wildlife. You will be funding our educational, legislative, investigative and outreach projects in the U.S. and across the globe.

Or perhaps you'd like to make a memorial donation in honor of a pet, friend or relative? You can through our Kindred Spirits program. And if you'd like to contribute in a more structured way, our Planned Giving Office has suggestions about estate planning, annuities, and even gifts of stock that avoid capital gains taxes.

Maybe you have land that you would like to preserve as a lasting habitat for wildlife. Our Wildlife Land Trust can help you. Perhaps the land you want to share is a backyard—that's enough. Our Urban Wildlife Sanctuary Program will show you how to create a habitat for your wild neighbors.

So you see, it's easy to help animals. And The HSUS is here to help.

The Humane Society of the United States
2100 L Street NW
Washington, DC 20037
202-452-1100
www.hsus.org

Chapter 3: Do Not Touch That Bank Account 49

Chapter 4: Living on Borrowed Dimes 61

Chapter 5: Negotiating with Sellers to Get the Financing You Need 71

Chapter 6: Using the Investor's Money and Credit   81

Chapter 7: Options Are Gold   93

Chapter 8: So You Want to Be a Landlord   101

Chapter 9: Finding Deals in Vacation Rentals, Foreclosures, and Subject-to Deals   109

Chapter 10: The Financing You Need   123

Chapter 11: The Undesirable Properties   157

Chapter 12: How to Find the Money You Need   165

Chapter 13: How to Promote Sales 195

Chapter 14: On the Contrary, I Am Speculating Successfully 205

Foreword

Most people work hard all their lives, save some money, and are disappointed in their lifestyle if they are finally able to retire. Many people today are worried about their own retirement, especially with the much-publicized woes of the social security system, and with fewer and fewer companies offering secure pensions. Some people dream of a better life—a life filled with an abundance of wealth and free from worry. Only a few people take the necessary actions to make their dreams a reality.

Napoleon Hill said, "Whatever the mind of man can conceive and believe it can achieve."[1]

Most people will never be able to achieve great levels of wealth merely by saving money. Sure, if you start early enough, earn an above-average income, live frugally, and save prodigiously, you can create a comfortable retirement. Nevertheless, most people will not figure all this out early enough in life. Most will need

---

[1]Napoleon Hill, *Think & Grow Rich* (New York City, New York: Ballantine Books, 1983), 32..

to find some method of using leverage if they are ever to build assets and cash flows sufficient to power a wealthy lifestyle in retirement.

Leverage is one of the most important tools used in the building of every great fortune. Using other people's money and other people's time will enable you to do exponentially more than you could ever do by yourself.

This book shows you many of the ways successful investors have literally created "something out of nothing" — and the ways you can do the same thing for you and your family.

I know these techniques work because I have used some of them myself.

When my wife and I purchased our first home, we had no money saved for the required down payment. Therefore, we used creative financing to purchase the home. As the home appreciated, we began to grow our net worth for the first time ever.

A couple of years later, we wanted to begin buying rental properties, yet we still did not have excess cash. Again, we used creative financing, this time obtaining owner financing from the seller.

We kept using various forms of creative financing for our subsequent purchases, even after the earnings from our first investments would have made it easy to buy without using creative techniques.

Why? Because creative financing offers so many advantages. For example, when you have no financial investment (or a very small one) the rate of return can be phenomenal. Additionally, creative financing often can save you money, either by minimizing closing costs, getting a lower interest rate, or negotiating other favorable terms. And of course, you can build your wealth so much more quickly when you can buy more properties, and this is much easier when you use creative financing. You too can reach tremendous levels of success through real estate investing.

Leverage is incredibly powerful, and it can either help you or hurt you. Susan Alvis shows throughout this book how important it is to use these techniques wisely and judiciously. If you do this, you will be able to smile as you watch your wealth growing safely and securely. One day, when many of your peers are still working just to survive, you will be enjoying the good life in a very secure retirement.

Norm Biller
President, The Biller Homes Team

Norm Biller leads one of the highest producing real estate consulting and sales teams in Lexington, Kentucky. He is also a real estate investor. He holds a Kentucky real estate broker's license.

Preface

Years ago entrepreneurs invested in real estate using traditional measures and that is all they knew how to do. Buying real property meant paying cash for it or financing it. If someone without cash wanted to buy a home or piece of land, he or she simply went to the local bank and borrowed the money. It was the way to do business when you wanted to purchase any real property. Not anymore. While the majority of investors and home buyers still go to a bank or mortgage company to borrow money, more people are discovering the art of the creatively financed real estate deal.

If the buyer wants to buy the property that the seller wants to sell, they can work together to make it happen by using creatively financed deals; something anyone can do by just taking the time to learn how. As a real estate agent in the '90s, I learned my job was to bring buyers and sellers together as quickly and effectively as possible, but one thing was always evident: if either one of the parties decided not to compromise, the deal died. When creatively financing properties, both buyer and seller must work toward an amicable goal of closing a property. Most of the time, when you have a would-be deal fall short of the closing table, it is because one or both parties refused to come together.

Smart investors know what it takes to take a deal to the closing table no matter which side of the table they happen to be sitting on at the time. You see, sharp investors will do what it takes to make everything come together because they like to buy and sell. They like to "trade" in real property. They are similar to many of the investors you would find on Wall Street. Real estate investors know as long as they are turning properties and watching those properties close at a closing table, they are turning money and that can mean big profits. Investors who are willing to work together will not waste time getting the deal to work. Why waste their time when they could easily be adding up their profits?

Creative financing for investors and homeowners is much easier today than in the past. Today, deals close with more frequency using a purchase-money mortgage. It is easier to get a bank and seller to work together to provide the lending package and if not, a mortgage company is on every corner. Plus you have the dot coms to fall back on, too. The future of lending lies in the virtual world and many of the businesses on the net are already becoming a mainstay.

When I sold real estate in the '90s, lending was much different. While the Internet was on the rise, finding reputable companies you could trust on the web was questionable. Now, there is a great lender to be found anytime you need one and they are really only a click away.

Today, investors are fortunate. They have so many tools they can use which can help them in their business. They can use the Internet to perform searches which can enable them to do their own comparative market analysis (CMA), check interest rates, find homes for sale all over the country, watch for FSBOs (and actually be alerted when one meets their needs), and so much more.

There have been more changes for the better only recently. The fact that many people used to have to go to the closing table with anywhere from 5 percent to 20 percent of their own cash was enough to stop potential investors in their tracks. Creatively financing real estate took off after the famous late night infomercials of Carlton Sheets ran rampant. Sheets not only *told* people how to do it but he *showed* them. Some even followed his suggestions and amassed wealth. Many investors had never heard of "no-money-down" and had never really formed any ideas about the creatively financed package. Some sellers could not fathom why anyone, as a homeowner would want to finance a property for someone they did not know. The entire concept of seller-financing seemed risky.

Sheets and investors who followed him showed people how creative financing could be done and laid out the money trail. On TV infomercials, the viewing public saw case study after case study and slowly it became apparent: these methods of creatively financing properties indeed worked for someone. (Either that or there were several ordinary people being paid to stand in front of some magnificent homes claiming to own them.)

Live footage showed the woman, barely able to feed her children, start to accumulate properties. The young couple who would have been renting started growing their investments from their first year of marriage. Sheets showed investors how the multi-million dollar lifestyle was possible for a young couple in their early twenties. It made multi-level marketing look like child's play. The reason? Well, that was obvious. Sheets offered to put Americans back into their own dreams. He offered people a way to make a life for themselves out of something tangible, and his ideas and philosophies made sense.

Soon people began to practice what Sheets had preached. Creative financing became common practice in real estate. Investors really started to shake things up a bit. It became obvious investors who wanted to buy properties would soon find a way to leave banks and traditional forms of financing to someone else. Why should they finance purchases through a traditional lender if they had a seller willing to be their banker? Creative financing had taken hold in the marketplace.

Now individuals know how to use someone else's money and credit to finance real estate purchases. They know how to profit from foreclosures and deal with judgments and liens. They use wraparound mortgages and second mortgages to find the money they need in their real estate dealings. In a word, real estate investors today are savvy. They watch the world markets and take notes. They study the trends and find out what outside forces will affect the housing sector. They gather information and then they use it to buy and sell when it's most advantageous.

The reason real estate investors are so savvy is because they have learned how to build a fortune based on solid assets. They know how to use little of their own cash to build wealth beyond anyone's wildest dreams. Best of all; they are able to find a way to accumulate wealth while helping others do the same by owner-financing their properties to other investors and first-time home buyers. They rent-to-own their properties and carry the paper on the homes they sell. They have learned how to be more than a landlord and are earning more money than ever before.

The neat thing about some of these talented individuals is that they are really able to walk away from what many of us consider an ordinary job and build a career from home. They work when they want to work and have built a legitimate, productive business right under their own roof tops.

How to Creatively Finance Your Real Estate Investments and Build Your Personal Fortune: What Smart Investors Need to Know –Explained Simply is going to be your reference as you embark on a new way to invest in real estate. This book will help you find a smarter way to sell and put more money in your pocket quickly. It will help you prepare as you creatively finance your properties and begin to build a real estate fortune. You can use the tools in the Appendix as you begin to offer your properties for sale to other buyers who are in search of homes using creative financing. You will find most of your questions are answered as you begin to accumulate investments of substance. Below, you'll see where this book is going to lead you.

In Chapter 1 we will look at the way the real estate market used to work. We will explore how people used to depend on the wisdom and the funds of the traditional lender when they were buying and selling their investments. Then, we will look at new and more creative ways to finance your investment properties.

In Chapter 2 we will delve into why it is important to use a real estate agent even when your goal is to finance your property through a seller or to find properties that are not typically agent-listed. You will discover real estate agents who know market trends and are up-to-date on your local market, can actually save you money and uncover properties for you. We will look at why you may want to have a real estate agent in your corner.

We will look at financing your investment properties with as little of your own money as possible in Chapter 3. We will glance at the preliminary steps you should take before you buy a property such as credit repair and budgeting for your investment properties. We will discuss the expenses involved in handyman specials, and I will show you how you can tidy up your fixer-upper with as little of your own cash as possible. You will even discover how to buy your investment holdings with no money down.

In Chapter 4, we will view how you can literally invest on borrowed dimes. We will take a look at how savvy investors are using funds and credit of willing participants to finance their investments while offering outsiders the chance to make money on their real estate transactions. We will discuss loans and fees associated with buying and selling real estate and show you what to expect when you go to the closing table.

Chapter 5 will explain how to negotiate with sellers to finance the property you want to buy creatively. We will take a glimpse at why it is important to get a seller in your corner so you can write winning proposals that your bank or lender will like. We will look at the best way to write winning offers-to-purchase worthy of a seller's consideration while helping you secure more creatively financed deals.

Chapter 6 takes a serious look at using the investor's money and credit. We will look at the reasons an outside investor will want to help you and how to use the credit-worthy businessman to help you get what you want, while allowing them to profit also. You will learn different ways to use the real estate entrepreneur to finance your ventures. In short, you will create a win-win situation for everyone.

Chapter 7 will teach you everything you need to know about options. You will understand the best ways to use them, how to approach the seller with an option, and how to sell the properties you buy on options before you actually buy them.

By the time you reach Chapter 8, you will feel like an old pro. We explore where to find the best deals for rental income. We will take a look at how to turn a tenant into a home owner and the best way you can do this. We will discuss lease-options and rent-to-owns as well as purchase-money mortgages. You will be able to find the best way to help your tenants while helping yourself to a never-ending flow of cash.

Chapter 9 looks at subject-to deals and foreclosures and how to make them work for you. We will look at how to find foreclosures and discuss real estate owned (REO). You will discover how foreclosures and subject-to deals work and how they can help you profit. This chapter will show you things to watch for in foreclosure deals and provide hints on how to maximize your profits when dealing with these investments.

In Chapter 10 you will learn how to secure the financing you need. We will take a look at various loans and mortgages and learn how to find the best way to finance your real estate investments. This chapter shows you where to find the money and how to call off a deal gone bad when it will cost you more in the long run to own it.

Undesirable properties will be discussed in Chapter 11. We look at properties that are over-financed and covered in liens. We discuss judgments and how working with undesirables can be profitable. You will see why buying "damaged by reputation" real estate can place even more cash in your hand.

Chapter 12 discusses the hidden places you can find more of your own money. You will learn about your 401(k) and IRA and how each of these can help you when funds are tight. Short-term loans are discussed in this chapter, and we look at which of these should be avoided. Finally, this chapter will help you see how to bring it all together when you are financing one property using several different methods.

In Chapter 13 I will show you how you can be an attractive seller. You will learn how to finance properties creatively for buyers using the best approaches. We discuss how the creative buyer is the best buyer you can hope to have as a seller when you are carrying some of the paper. Discover why finding the best agent to market your properties can be crucial when you are a seller just waiting for the right action!

Finally in Chapter 14, we look at the goals of the investor who does everything apart from the norm. We take a quick look at why real estate gurus are making it to the top of this business by doing the exact opposite of what many traditional real estate businessmen have done in the past.

This book is the guide you need to teach you more about creatively financing your real estate investments while building wealth whether you are the seller or the buyer. You are provided with a solid foundation as you begin to invest in the greatest commodity in the world — real estate.

I wrote this book for you — the investor. My hope is you will use this book to begin building a real estate fortune without procrastinating. Donald Trump once said, "It is tangible, it is solid, it is beautiful, it is artistic from my standpoint, and I just love real estate." I am going to show you how you can love real estate too and how you can own something "solid and tangible" using creative measures to obtain as much of it as you want to own.

Chapter One

The Way Things Were Many Moons Ago

I used to hear old-timer stories from the investors I dealt with in real estate. They were proud that they had the money and the brains to lock themselves into real estate investments. Some of them even regretted not jumping into real estate earlier. When real estate holdings were discussed, most of them had a strong opinion about how they were able to obtain their small (or vast) fortunes based on their early decisions.

If you ever discuss real estate with an older investor, you will likely find yourself hearing how much property cost back in the '50s or '60s. You will think to yourself, "Wow, if only I had been able to invest then." These investors paint a picture of affordable real estate and easy banking where the good ol' boys could shake hands and close a deal. However, history shows it was not that simple. In fact, if it had been that simple, a lot more of old family money would have come down the heritage lines. As you look around your own communities, you can probably see this was not usually the case.

The fact is, compared to today's prices, real estate in the '50s and '60s was cheap, but it was regarded as pricey and out of reach for many. What sounds like cheap real estate to us often cost the individual a much overtime and personal sacrifice to obtain. Still, real estate was the place to deposit any extra money you could find and if you did not have it, then you could visit your friendly banker who would gladly lend you what he could.

To give you an idea of how things were back in the '50s, I talked to my father-in law, Bill Alvis, about how things really were back in the day. Bill has been in the home building supply industry for more than 40 years and knows how things were back then.

$15,000 does not sound like much money

Bill Alvis
Alvis-Kilby Lumber
Tri-Cities, Tennessee

In the late '50s, a 26 × 48 home (1,248 square feet) would cost a person about $15,000 to build. Adding in the labor, someone building a home could expect to spend a total of about $21,000. It would cost someone about $35,000 to buy a 26 × 48 house. Keep in mind; this does not include the lot. You would expect to pay another $3,500–$5,000 for your lot depending on the size of the lot.

to build a nice 1,200 square-foot home, but it was then. Banks were stringent about extending credit. Imagine what would have happened if creative financing without traditional lenders had been typical then. Many average people would have ended up with above average bank accounts and while some did, most did not.

In those days, the businessmen who owned property were not using creative means to purchase the property they bought. The people who had taken the steps to make astonishing passive incomes through bold speculation were not familiar with creative financing. At least, they were not using measures we use now to finance real estate purchases creatively. Instead, these guys were using cold hold cash and the assistance of their local banker.

People depended on the wisdom of their community banker to help them finance their residence. Farmers would talk to Farm Credit, for example, in hopes of securing financing for their farm and land dreams. Often the banker would sit on his perch and make strong recommendations regarding this person when discussing financing with a loan committee. In many towns there was no committee, only the banker.

Fortunately for us, things have moved forward, and investors and homeowners no longer have to depend solely on their local banks for financing. Sometimes it is best to go to a bank, but other times it is more advantageous to find financing elsewhere or with only a small percentage of funds coming from the bank. After all, creatively financing real estate purchases has given clever minds assets far beyond their normal incomes.

There is much to be said for this country's real estate millionaires. They are investing in something solid. They are placing their money and time in a worthy commodity. After all, there is no hope for more land to be produced. At least, no one has mentioned it!

Take a look at the information my father-in-law provided above. In 1959 a 1,200 square-foot home sold for $35,000. Today, that same home will range from $120,000 to more than $200,000 if it is in the suburbs of a thriving city. What do you think will happen in another 25–35 years? If real estate continues to follow a trend and history repeats itself, the value of real estate will continue to rise. It only makes sense for everyone to begin accumulating as much of it as possible because if we don't, years down the road our children will wonder why we didn't!

In a few years, the questions you may have asked your own parents and grandparents may come back to you full circle. Your children will wonder why you failed to buy up as much real estate as you could buy. Will you have answers for them?

With today's new way to buy and sell real property, you will have no excuse for not buying. Poor credit, bad credit, or no credit will not stop you from becoming a property owner. Even the lack of money will not hold you back. Today's financiers of real estate holdings will finance just about anyone. They know they can take the steps they need to take to ensure their vested interests are secure.

The reason that this moment is *almost* the perfect time for you to begin acquiring property has everything to do with our history and past trends that generally repeat the same patterns. Even when prices of real estate holdings are strong in most places, the trends of the past would indicate it would be time for the market to take a turn downward. When it does, it will be a prime time to buy.

With all the outstanding opportunities to finance real estate purchases creatively you can begin to finance your real estate investments using some of the methods discussed throughout this book. It can start with your own home and lead to investments such as apartment buildings and small rental homes. You can creatively finance mobile home parks and retail strip malls or hotels and bed and breakfasts. Whatever you want to buy, you can find a way to do it with creative financing in place.

The Old Way of Doing Business

You can wait to begin purchasing real estate after you become financially secure, but if you wait, you will pay more for the properties you buy. If you wait, you miss out on some good things in life because you are not building wealth. Money may not buy happiness, but it makes life easier and it can create a stable future for those you love.

When my children were both under five years old, we were planning to go to the beach. Someone advised my husband that we could not afford to go to the beach because we had bills to pay, so we did not go. Would you like to know how many memories we missed out on because he listened to someone he thought was wise? We missed out on many of them and the thing is, those opportunities were just there for the taking one time. The same holds true for real estate investments. If you wait until you can afford to make them, you will miss out on opportunities and you will miss out on the income.

Today, real estate investments are easy to obtain. Excellent credit is not a prerequisite: you do not even need credit to buy real estate and, best of all; you do not need a hefty balance in your bank accounts. Keep in mind though; the people who are accumulating real estate are quietly doing it without traditional lenders. They are not coming up with the 5 percent to 20 percent down payment required by some of the lending institutions. They are using other methods. These new-age entrepreneurs are talking with sellers and other potential investment partners to find ways to afford properties they want.

The old way of doing business in real estate meant you needed cash or you needed better credit than half the town where you wanted to buy property. You would not just find a wealthy seller and ask him to carry the financing because in those days, that would be almost as woeful as begging for help from a stranger. Still, there were those who put their money in the right investments and their strategies paid off. Never mind the fact these people were *unable* to put any money down.

The theme of the day back then was that the rich became wealthier and the poor remained poor. The more investment properties the banks saw these people owned, the more interested in the investor the banker became. If you did not have the money to buy your first home, you were expected to rent from one of the lucky guys who owned lots of property in the area. Anyone could tell you who the landlords were because everyone knew them.

Family money would give the wealthy an "in" with the banks and lenders—one reason affluent families were able to buy up so much real estate. However, for everyone else owning a home would not come easy until the age of the baby boomers. They learned to use credit and it was easier for them to buy property. Ownership suddenly came within reach and could be secured.

Baby boomers were followed by Generation X, and what a mess things have been for the generation as a whole! This generation faced dilemmas early on because credit was extended much easier than to any other generation in the form of credit cards. Most of Generation X claimed their fist-full of credit cards while in college and what a great time we had using them. It was not uncommon to see that the credit extended eventually prevented financial growth. After all, this credit was used for cars, furniture, trips, and other right-now necessities. No one stopped to think about an investment or a roof over their head.

When reality finally set in among these two generations and the banks and finance companies that had been the enablers, mortgage companies became more competitive. It became their job to help finance dreams and even then, the credit-ridden couples of the early '90s could not afford to buy. It became evident creative financing would be the only way for many couples to finance their dreams, and Carlton Sheets and his infomercials taught people how to do it.

The Down Payment of Years Gone By

Talk about creative financing with some of the older investors of the day and they may look at you like you are out of your mind. They had used cash to buy their investments and if not, they still had a sizeable down payment when they started to invest in properties other than their primary residence.

Typically, when an investor started out, he worked night and day to pay off the first property and then he acquired a second. Occasionally, there were exceptions but generally speaking it was all work and little play to secure a future with real estate holdings.

Now if you cannot afford to buy something, banks and mortgage companies just recalculate and do some minor adjustments — which always cost the borrower in the end — and then hocus-pocus, you have yourself a loan that you cannot afford to pay. That just did not happen years ago, but it does now. Financing makes it possible to afford whatever it is you really cannot afford. Creative financing does the same thing except that you can control it and make it work to your advantage.

Once you are in control, you have the power to see great things begin to happen. You have the flexibility you need to begin to acquire more properties and you begin to look pretty good on a piece of paper. This is when you begin to see how creative financing can be attractive.

Dealing with Banks and Mortgage Companies

In the old days; deals were as simple as a handshake but an entirely different story when it came down to financing the deals that were made. People would find a home they wanted to buy, give a good faith binder on the house or land if necessary, and trot off to the local bank to see what their own banker had to say.

The faith people put into their local banks and institutions such as Farm Credit was unbelievable. People depended on the banker's wisdom for advice. If the banker told them they had poor credit or could not afford a loan, they informed the seller they simply "could not come up with the money." Banks were like the parent who issued permission to their children but, fortunately, now they have more competition forcing them to be impartial whereas before, the favorite child often received the nod of approval. Creative financing has enabled the credit-defunct or credit-disabled home investor to invest and beat all odds while becoming successful as a real estate speculator.

Interest Rates

Now we have options for obtaining money for a real estate purchase, for interest rates, and for what we are willing to pay. If the seller is the banker, options are a little more diverse. If not, you still have options on where to find the money and how much you are willing to pay for the use of it.

When a person looks outside local lenders for financing, usually it is because of high interest rates and the loan terms and conditions. When someone finds loan options outside of normal sources, he or she can sometimes catch a seller or investor willing to lower their rates. The seller or private lender may work out a payment schedule including balloon payments. House payments may be made quarterly. In short, the seller and the buyer come together on terms that meet the needs of both parties.

On the other side of the lending war, you have a big entity weighing heavily. When the Federal Reserve meets to discuss rates, they consider several outside sources when making a decision. National elections, wars, and any major changes in the big board (stocks) can certainly play a part in the decisions at these meetings. If you borrowed money on an adjustable interest rate, you probably pay attention to these meetings and the news following them.

Creative financed homeowners are unaffected during "bad" times because they are typically locked in at an interest rate. They know the volatility in real estate but, are not easily shaken by it. After all, when a housing market is said to be "bad" or "slow" it is declining. In many other industries, when it is bad, it could mean it is crashing — yet another reason the housing market is such a great place for your money. If you own property and the economy is failing, chances are it will regain momentum and you can hold onto it until it does. If you do not want to hold, you can often sell using creative measures and always find a buyer who wants to become a homeowner. In a worst case scenario, you can even rent it at a discount but at least it is not a total loss. Other sectors can be devastated so badly it is hard to bounce back.

Real estate is safer than most investment choices. However, it is the people who invest as contrarians who are able to thrive. The contrarian is the investor who is willing to take a stand against what the masses would view as general knowledge. Donald Trump is a prime example. He would go into areas most people would not dare to go and make a fortune from the outset.

As you begin to finance your investments creatively, you will become more like a contrarian because you will be going into areas of financing most would not dare to go. You will find the financing package you want, the one to meet your needs, anywhere you can find it and when you do, you will be able to begin building a portfolio of real estate to be envied.

I am not suggesting that you never go to a bank. Sometimes banks are hard to beat on their lending packages. For example, a jumbo loan package for large purchases can allow the borrower to catch a deal on their interest rate. Sellers would not want to match, in most cases, the low rate a lender may offer on a large loan. Still, it is suggested for all buyers to check out their options for financing before they hand over their business to any lending institution. In many cases, the home owner will provide a much sweeter deal.

Taking the Creative Road to a Better Approach

Investors with good credit sometimes wonder if the creative approach to financing is the best. If the investor plans to purchase numerous properties, yes, absolutely! The more creative options used, the better because the entrepreneur is able to diversify and add to their holdings quicker. Even if the diversity falls in the grey area of financing, the more financing investors do creatively, the better off they are especially regarding a debt-to-income ratio. If a seller is holding a purchase money mortgage on a property for you, and you are not sure if your credit could carry the weight of two home loans, this is where the creative deal is appealing.

One of the main reasons investors begin financing their homes and real estate transactions through other investors and sellers is because it allows them more flexibility in their lending options. They can buy several properties and seem to a lender that they are overextended. Remember, even if paperwork shows that you are not over-extended, you can often be at the door of the poorhouse unless you take precautions to protect your investments. One way to do this is to make sure you are either quickly flipping the properties you buy or placing secure tenants in the homes you own.

Buyers who buy through their sellers and other private financiers should be aware of what they can afford. Many ages ago, a man who went to the bank for loan approval knew that if he was given the loan, he could afford the payment because it was based on his current income and situation. Today, if you are working within the realm of creatively financing your properties, you need to calculate your payments and expenses; otherwise, you will be unaware of how close you are to losing everything.

FOOD FOR THOUGHT

A young girl tried to get her husband to invest in ocean front condos but he refused. She invested without telling him. She bought several properties on the ocean on lease-purchase and realized a profit the first season as all three were leased steadily on a week by week basis and then month-to-month in the fall and winter. The second season, she was unlucky. She rented all three condos in the summer on a week by week status. However, when fall rolled around, only one condo rented for the fall and winter.

Since the condos were in a vacation area, she had to work two jobs the second season just to pay her lease on the condos until the vacation season rolled around again. Finally, she broke down and told her husband they held three condos on lease with the option to buy all three. He asked her if he was her "Plan B."

The woman in this scenario had good investment intentions. Her initial investments were on lease-option contracts. She was able to accumulate properties in several vacation areas using lease-options and rent-to-own contracts. The problem she faced was she did not have a "Plan B." When you begin to buy real estate using creative financing, no one will be there to talk to you about your debt-ratio or to show you what you can or cannot afford.

While using creative financing can allow you the opportunity to buy more properties at a much faster rate, you still need to buy what you can afford. What will you do when the properties you are buying are without tenants to pay the rent and help you with mortgage payments? Work a second job or lower rents? Will you let the investment home go back to the original seller and lose the equity you built up? What is your "Plan B?" When it comes to investing, you may need one!

Chapter Two

Finding the Perfect Property Using the Perfect Agent

F inding great properties can be time-consuming. No one really has the time to work a full time job, repair and remodel fixer-upper homes, take care of the family, and search for new properties to buy. Unless you have the good fortune to run across a good deal on your own by mere accident, you will need to search for the properties you want to buy. You have no time to search if you are a real estate investor actively working on turning or flipping real estate. Here we introduce the best way to invest—with the help of a real estate professional.

Many investors go it alone especially when they are looking for deals such as seller-financing or no-money-down opportunities. Even more of them try to place buyers in their properties under those same terms and never stop to consider a real estate agent might help make their job easier.

As a real estate agent, I worked with as many investors as I could. Most of them were willing to work with potential home buyers as their primary resident. Some of them were open to financing as many homes as they could afford so they could count on a monthly income from the property.

FOOD FOR THOUGHT

I discovered that, even if my commissions were delayed because of a lease-option or other creative form of financing, I preferred working with investors who were repeat clients. They knew what to expect from me and I knew what to expect from them.

Too often, new investors hesitate to work with real estate agents because of the cost. However, when you are an investor-seller you just work the commission into your sales price and when you are an investor-buyer, the seller pays the commission. Either way, an active real estate agent who knows he or she can depend on you in the future for other transactions should be glad to accept delayed commissions to earn your business.

Why Using a Real Estate Agent Works for Investors

Real estate agents love to work with investors. When you find a real estate agent you can trust, you quickly discover it is important to let an agent be your eyes and ears in the real estate community. Not only can they spot potential homes for you within the MLS (multiple listing service), but they can also keep you up to speed on things such as foreclosures, options, and other offerings which may be of interest to you.

Find a real estate agent who is a producer. I believe in giving a new agent a shot at your business if you really believe he or she is going to be a hard worker with your interests in mind. After all, I had several people take a chance on me when I was new in the business. However, often it is hard for a real estate investor to work with a new agent who is still learning the business and has few contacts. More experienced investors can certainly work with new agents and often help them along, but newer investors should work with more experienced realtors. A seasoned agent is not going to make the mistakes a new agent may make. New agents can cost the investor missed opportunities while they are still learning the business.

An agent can impart information you will not have otherwise, and if you are going to buy several properties in a fiscal year, you *need* an agent working for you. An agent can minimize your work load and in most cases you never pay the commission as a buyer. By shopping smart and investing wisely, the agents' commissions will be minimal when you sell compared to your bottom line profit on each deal. There are countless reasons to consider working with an agent.

Following are just some of the reasons an investor needs an agent:

- *An agent can find out about a new listing in the MLS which meets your needs.*
  Have you ever wondered how the other guy knows about good deals before the general public has the opportunity to find them? It pays to have someone on the inside because realtors are going to find out about the best deals around — the ones that never make it to the general public.

- *They will know about foreclosures and other properties in trouble.*
  There are many ways an agent finds out about a potential foreclosure before anyone else. Perhaps the office where the agent works receives a fax from a lender about a REO or maybe they just hear a rumor about a troubled property. Either way, you need an agent to look for these opportunities for you.

- *An agent will know about new subdivisions.*
  Should you decide to work with new home developments, you will want to be in the know when new subdivisions are on the rise. This way, you will have first dibs on the choice lots and often can work out a creative contract with a developer who needs to have builders in the subdivision as quickly as possible.

- *They will know about other investors looking for real estate partners.*
  Let agents know that you are interested in backing other investors financially. This is a good way to find other means of making money within the real estate world. The flip side of that is also to let an agent know you are interested in working with other investors when they are looking to provide the purse as well.

- *An agent will be able to line up home inspections, termite inspections, surveys, and appraisals when a loan officer is not involved. Even when a loan officer is involved, an agent will assist with these things.*
  Face it; an agent can save you money especially when you are turning over several properties, and they can save you time taking care of the details involved in buying or selling a home.

- *An agent will know inside information on certain properties.*
  An agent will tell you the morbid things you may not want to know but need to know just the same. If someone has died in the home, he or she will let you know — not that this should be a deterrent to your buying, but you should know for resale purposes.

- *A licensed real estate agent is a trained professional who will often see deterrents in a deal that you may not.*

An agent will know things you will not be aware of about certain properties. They are legally obligated to share with you what they know about a property you are interested in buying. Furthermore, they should be trained to be on the lookout for things such as obvious termite damage or a roof in poor condition.

- *They can save you steps by filtering through properties to find one to meet your needs.*

    When you have the money but not the time, an agent can comb through several of the properties listed to find the deal she or he knows will be a match for you.

- *Agents can help you with creative financing and often are key players in working a creative deal.*

    Realtors know their business and especially when their own commission is involved, they can find a way to help you get the financing you need even if it is just by making simple suggestions you may not have thought about. They have been on the sidelines enough to know what works.

- *They can ensure a deal makes it to the closing table to look over closing statements and documents enabling you just to show up at the closing, glance over the documents, sign, and go.*

    In short, real estate agents are worth their weight in gold! If you have ever viewed a settlement statement, you know these documents are not always simple to read or understand. Agents are paid to understand them and spot any potential red flags.

It is a real estate agent's job to make investing in real estate as easy as possible. Savvy agents know if they take care of your business transactions, they are making it easier for you and the easier it is for you; the more you will buy and sell through them.

Finding the Agent You Need for Your Goals

When I was an agent, I was fortunate to work with a handful of extremely loyal clients—whom I appreciated. A couple of them were smart enough to sit down with me at the beginning of our business relationship to tell me what it was they planned to do. We talked about their goals, needs, and what they generally expected from me. Investors who were mindful enough to take the time to discuss their needs were usually the easiest investors to please down the road. Agents should be willing to listen to you as their investor-client because you can become their bread and butter if both of you keep your goals in focus.

When looking for a realtor, find one who is willing to listen to what you are trying to do. Find someone who will recognize you as a long-term client with investment goals. Let them know you are planning for success with a road map that includes using them for direction. If they sense your loyalty, they will make every effort to keep your needs in mind. They will get in tune with your needs and your means of financing them.

As an investor, you need to take the time to interview a few real estate agents and let them know what you are looking for in an agent. Tell them your goals and what you expect them to do for you. The following items should be on the agenda.

- Discuss the expectations you have and why you are interviewing agents.

- Tell them what they can expect from you.

- Explain to them what kind of properties you want to buy.

- Talk to them about the price range you have in mind for the properties you acquire.

- Let them know the types of creative financing you are going to be using to buy the properties.

- Give them a rough estimate of how many properties you plan to buy and how soon you want to begin buying.

- You should also discuss paying them as a buyer's agent if there comes a time when they will not be benefiting much from their hard work.

Always be accessible to people who are your clients. Return their calls and answer their e-mails. You will find if you give attention to detail and are attentive to client needs, you will close more deals as a real estate agent.

Jay Crockett
Realty Executives
423-952-0226
www.tricitiesarearealestate.com

It is important to discuss exactly what you want your agent to do. Do you want the agent to pre-screen properties for you to find out whether the seller is open to creative financing? Do you want the agent to narrow down options and show you the best three

FOOD FOR THOUGHT

Larry owned a condominium complex with 30 units and worked a full-time job. By the time he pulled his 12-hour shift at a factory every day, he was tired but always had somewhere he needed to be at the complex. A water heater needed his attention one day and a broken window the next. He knew if he had time to look around, he could probably buy one more eight- or ten-unit complex and be ready to retire but he had no time to find the properties. He did not pursue it until he met an agent willing to do his legwork for him.

After he hired a real estate agent, not only did he find another 16 units but he also entered all his rental units into a property management program with the real estate agent's firm. Now he has time for to enjoy life and will be retiring soon.

properties within your price range when you look at homes or should they call you whenever they find one perfect for you?

When shopping for an agent, find someone you feel comfortable working with long-term who is open to working with you long-term. Find an agent who is professional as well as knowledgeable and knows the area better than most in his or her field.

A good agent in tune with their investor's needs learns quickly what their buyer wants to buy. It is common for investors to work with an agent and not hear from them for a couple of weeks or even a month until one day the phone rings and the voice on the other end announces, "Meet me at the office. I have found one." This is the kind of agent investors want. They want to know the agent will call them as soon as he or she finds the perfect property.

It is important to be an expert on the real estate trends in your area. Always know what property values are doing and what the average days on market are. You will find people are more inclined to work with you when you can provide them with the most information possible. You can learn market trends for your area by learning from experienced agent.

Jay Crockett
Realty Executives
423-952-0226
www.tricitiesarearealestate.com

What to Expect from Your Real Estate Agent

As an agent, I had several demanding clients but I must say the investors I worked with were simply the best. They told me what they wanted and expected me to go out and find it. They knew I would call them when I found what they wanted. As an investor, you need an agent who will just take care of your buying and selling business. They are representing you and in many cases, your agent will be an extension of you and your business when you are not available.

After you choose your agent, tell the person what you expect.

- Describe the first property you want to buy. Tell the agent how much you will pay and how the first one will be financed.

- Talk about your needs for the upcoming year so they will have an idea of where this business relationship is headed.

- Let the agent know what you are going to be doing with the property. Are you going to put the property back on the market after a couple of minor improvements? Do you plan to rent the property? What are your goals for property number one?

- If you are going rent the property, do you need the agent to handle leasing your rentals? If so, you will need to discuss the leasing contract you want and what the agent can expect to earn. How much will you pay the agent to be your property manager or will you be paying the agent's firm?

- How much work do you expect from your agent? Are you going to leave a big portion of the decision-making process up to your agent or do you want her to call you when she has several properties lined up for you to view? How will your agent-client relationship work? Leave nothing to chance; discuss it.

You need to tell your agent how soon you hope to buy. If you are eager to get started and feel that you are running a marathon in a sprint to the closing table with property number one, tell your agent. Even if you are in no hurry, let your agent know you are looking to buy your first investment property within a set number of weeks so they get that sense of urgency and start searching for you.

How to Find the Best Property for Your Goals

There are many opportunities for investors and there is really no way to know the best place to start. You can break into your investments by starting out with fixer-upper, or you may prefer to start out buying small houses where most of the work has already been done. You can flip the property for a quick sale, or you can become a landlord and rent it. You can even buy some properties to flip and some to rent. In this business, you have loads of options.

As a new real estate investor, give some thought to the kind of properties you want to buy. Before buying them, you will need to define your short-term and long-term goals for the properties. Otherwise, you will not be able to make the money as quickly as you want to make it.

Obviously, there are vast differences in many of the properties you buy. You may want to buy land to develop or just stick with handy-man specials. Whatever your goals, you will achieve them if you have a plan in effect and you make the decision to work your plan. Use your real estate agent to plan your year of transactions. Find out where the good deals are. Ask your agent to prepare a comparative market analysis for you on properties you want to see. Learn the market in the areas where you will be buying and selling. Ask questions and gain as much knowledge as you can.

Get to know some loan officers in the area. Even though you are going to be looking at creative measures to finance your real estate purchases, you never know when you may get a deal through. Understand even when you use creative methods, the way you finance may include using a bank or traditional lender.

Try to have one mortgage company and one bank you are able to work with amicably so they become familiar with you and you with them.

What You Need to Know to Make Smart Investments

As you begin to make your investments, you will learn about many different methods of financing. Talk to your real estate agent for suggestions on creative financing and take notes as you go through this book. Often a beginning real estate investor will have no idea about financing outside traditional lending. Unless you have a mortgage lending or real estate background, you probably will not know much about the various ways you can finance your purchases but you will after you read up on your options and practice what you read.

Here are a few key points to share with your agent before you begin to buy using creative methods.

1. You want a property capable of producing cash flow or the potential for cash flow.

2. You will be interested in how fast a property will appreciate over time. Whether the property is producing income, you want a sound investment where the property value will appreciate.

3. You want to yield the highest return possible on your investment.

4. You want creative financing so you will always be interested in the seller who is interested in providing it.

Finally, let the real estate agent know that you will be buying as the contrarian investor, meaning you will often make your investment move by going against what is considered typical. Tell the agent that while you value his or her expertise, you find it crucial to go against what everyone else is doing.

You want results to be evident by seeing profits and since you invest in a manner that typically scoffs at conventional wisdom, some of your moves will not necessarily look like risk-free plays. Still, using your approaches to buy and sell real property, you will be confident that the direction you choose to take is sound.

Whatever you do, take time to coach your agent on your investing approach. If you are definitely going to follow the contrarian mind set, tell your realtor what this means for you and for them. Coach them on the contrarian ways. Make sure the agent understands in many cases you will learn from their advice and yet move in the opposite direction in hopes of higher profitability.

Chapter Three

Do Not Touch That Bank Account

We know if more people had more money, fewer people would be renters. We know this because we know people who rent. Most of us at some point in our lives have rented a home or an apartment. Why? Because we either did not have the money to buy or we were renting for a short-term plan based usually on saving for a long-term investment. It is doubtful we did it just to help out a friendly landlord. The fact is that unless someone is in between homes — which is often the case with buyers building a new home — renters become renters because they cannot afford to become owners, plain and simple.

Many renters would be buying their first home right now if they knew more about creatively financing their purchase. In fact, if you are renting right now and you want to buy a home, good news is in store for you! Regardless of your current or past financial history, income, or even your current credit score, there is a good chance someone out there is willingly to finance your real estate purchase.

Renters can become instant investors if they will just take the initiative to learn more about how to do it. Sometimes a landlord will open a window of opportunity by providing a way for his investors to buy from him. He will grant his tenants a rent-to-own contract and show them how easy it can be to become a homeowner.

FOOD FOR THOUGHT

Two young couples start out in life at about the same time. One couple immediately shows promise and finds a condominium in the city with an agreeable seller who is more than willing to provide the couple with some creative options for financing. They borrow the down payment and finance their condo on a purchase-money mortgage with the seller. Their payments are affordable and they are building equity.

Another young couple finds a home in a subdivision they cannot afford. The young woman wants her friends to admire her new status in life and so her husband reluctantly agrees to move into the subdivision. They lock into a two-year lease with a $1,400 rent hanging over their head each month on a property they will never own. At the end of the second year, a baby is on the way and the young couple decides to stay where they are because they know they cannot save for a home with $1,400 in rent going out each month.

Five years later, couple number one begins to search for an investment property while couple number two can barely make ends meet. Couple number one dreams of owning more investment properties, and they seem to enjoy life while couple number two has no dream of every owning a home of their own. Divorce begins to loom and as far as either party is concerned, it cannot be soon enough.

The scenario on the previous page is written only for illustrative purposes. Young couples do make dreadful financial mistakes similar to the ones couple number two made and when there is no money for fun activities or a sound and secure future, one part of the not-so-happy couple splits in search of a better life. Who could blame them?

Young couples who want to be homeowners can find a better way to start their lives together without going into debt. They can begin their new lives in a small rent-to-own condo or buy a house using a lease-option. These young people have alternatives to traditional lending without having to worry about time on the job or anything else. Sellers are standing by to offer creative terms!

The Other Guy's Dough

As you begin to invest, learn how to finance those acquisitions without digging deep into your own pockets. While you may initially feel that you are imposing on the seller, consider the following and think again:

In creative financed deals, most of the time the seller wants you to use them as your lender.

I am going to teach you how to use the seller as well as traditional and other private lenders to help you understand how to finance your investments. I want you to know how to use your 401(k), options, the seller's money, and many different types of mortgages. If you want to invest, you need to learn all the best ways to do it with as little of your own money as possible. We will even tell you about the subject-to deals and how to capitalize on foreclosures before they hit the auction block.

FOOD FOR THOUGHT

Cara and John wanted to buy a new home but with only $3,000 to their name. The likelihood seemed a distant dream until one day John read in the newspaper that a seller of a two-bedroom home was entertaining all offers and would consider owner financing. He could not wait to see the house. He was sure he would be interested in buying if the seller could work with them.

The couple drove out to a little subdivision in their rural community and met with the seller who told them he was firm on his price of $50,000 and he would be willing to finance the whole thing if they would pay the closing costs. Cara and John fell in love with the house and they came to terms on the interest rate. They made 60 payments of $955.05 and 5 years later owned their home free of any liens.

Initially, John had felt a little intimidated about allowing the seller to finance. Even though the seller was a willing participant and the initiating party of the arrangement, John felt the older gentleman could have sold the place outright. However, what John did not see was the larger picture.

The home the young couple bought was an older house in a subdivision in the middle of nowhere. Because the home had only 950 square feet, $50,000 was a top price. Since the owner financed the property, the buyers did not have an appraisal on the home but of course, this saved them the additional tab on their closing costs. The slick businessman not only received about $4,200 more than the house was worth but he also earned another $7,303.48 in interest so in the end he was well compensated for his troubles.

While using all your assets can always be an option, I hope you will avoid digging into your 401(k) and selling stock unless you are sure the profit potential warrants it. Investors commonly pull money from their stocks and other investments to pay down payments and closing costs. While this is fine to do and you should use all means at your disposal when you are trying to work a transaction, you want to be sure you are not penalized to the point your profit is invaded. In most cases, there are easier ways to make a good real estate deal.

Savvy real estate speculators reduce their risk to ensure they finance their purchases the best way they can. How? They use someone else's money and sometimes even their credit!

Real estate is an investor's dream because it carries less risk than most investments, and it offers more security. However, investing in real estate often takes more cash *up front* than any other investment. That is why being a creative investor is important: you will quickly discover how to buy property with little of your own capital invested on the front end, enabling you to make profitable decisions.

Preparing Yourself for Smart Investing

In *How to Buy Real Estate without a Down Payment in Any Market*, I showed you how to prepare yourself for a credit-worthy appearance to lenders. If you read the book, you saw how to clean up your credit so you looked more appealing to traditional lenders. I recommend you read the book if you have poor credit.

In the book we talked about the best ways to buy without money or credit and, believe it or not, many people quickly discovered these ideas indeed worked!

FOOD FOR THOUGHT

Carla had everything in order when she walked into my office: copies of her credit report, billing statements, and everything she thought we might need to see. She had itemized everything they owed and listed cash on hand as well as their other assets. I was meeting with Carla and Dave before the mortgage broker met with them and I did not glance at any of her paperwork because their loan officer had told me the couple had pre-qualified for a $150,000 house. Carla and I chatted about what she wanted in a home and I was impressed at how prepared she was. I do not think I ever had a client any more prepared or any more excited to buy a house than she was.

Dave, her husband, arrived in a beautiful shiny red Corvette. Since the sports car was my all-time favorite car, I went out to have a look and noticed the look of defeat on Carla's face. We chatted for a few minutes about how the car handled and how he paid a pretty penny for it. He was proud of his new purchase but Carla was seething.

Carla was teary-eyed by the time we sat down and I pretended not to notice as it dawned on me why she would have such a change in demeanor. As the couple talked, I saw a sale going straight out the door. During the time Carla had been diligently working on the couple's credit, Dave discovered they had excellent credit that looked better on paper than he had thought. In three days, he had bought a sports car, a camper, and a boat. It was nothing short of amazing but given the fact he was only 22 at the time, I chalked it up to immaturity and assured Carla these things could be sold quickly after he had a chance to play with his boy toys. It did not help matters.

CONTINUED

The couple did stay long enough for me to run some preliminary numbers for them, but ultimately they left before the loan officer arrived. After all, they quickly saw they would not qualify for a home loan or at least the kind of house they wanted to buy. Needless to say, I never saw them in my office again.

We talked about the image borrowers present to lenders. Do you know how you would look to lenders and mortgage brokers if you wanted to buy a house right now? Smart investors know they need to look good on paper. However, you might be surprised to know some of the richest people in the business of buying and selling real estate were completely broke at least once before they began to accumulate real estate assets. What many people have a tough time wrapping their mind around is this. Even if you have absolutely no money, you can begin not only to invest in real estate but become financially stable doing it. However, you need to become real estate focused. You want to learn to make good business decisions and use the creative methods cautiously so you never get in over your head.

Investors who are focused on their goals of investing in real estate know they need to clean up their credit if they have some tardy payments messing up their credit score. They understand frivolous spending with credit cards or additional loans can be viewed as a negative by lenders. Most of the time, if they do not realize it going into the real estate speculation, they soon will. Serious players in real estate do not make foolish choices by clouding up their credit and debt-to-income with frivolous spending because they never know when they may need their credit in tip top shape.

One of the first steps you should make once you decide real estate investing is for you is to clean up and then maintain your credit report. Check out your own credit report to see if everything on it is accurate. Should any red flags catch your attention, you should immediately take measures to correct it.

After you make sure you look like a credit worthy buyer, you will want to know how lenders view your credit. It is never a bad idea to meet with a loan officer just to see how a lender would perceive a loan application from you. Usually this can be accomplished through a pre-qualification process and this is one of the best ways to discover how you rate with traditional lenders!

Banks and Loan Officers

When you sit down with a mortgage loan officer, talk to them openly about your goals and current financial situation. However, do not give away too much if you are only sitting down for some free advice. Loan officers want you to obtain your lending package from them and they are not particularly concerned with giving away free advice on how to finance your home through creative measures. Of course, if you are a regular customer of the bank or you send steady business to the lender, they may be happy to provide you with information.

Ask your loan officer for some input of their own. See what programs and loan packages they offer for investors. If you can find a loan company or locally owned bank, you may find possibilities right in your hometown branch. However, with large banks gobbling up smaller ones, often the friendly hometown service is gobbled right along with the structure. Still, if you are lucky enough to find a friendly, knowledgeable loan officer, you can learn from suggestions they offer.

Something you should get into the habit of doing when you meet with lenders is to find out all you can about the bank's inventory of REO. When you meet with your bank or loan officer, you need to let them know you are interested in buying foreclosed properties. Now would also be a good time to find out what the loan officer knows about the lender's REO (real estate owned) properties in their own bank or at other area banks and mortgage companies.

Keep in mind the best time for you to locate REO properties is right before they go to the real estate agency to be sold as REO and definitely before they reach the auction block as foreclosures. So anytime you meet with someone in the banking industry, it is ideal to ask for their input on where to find the best selection of REO properties. Who knows, you may get lucky and be told about one you cannot refuse.

As a speculator who will be looking for properties to buy creatively, you need to learn to ask questions all the time. When talking to lenders, you want to ask them what they can do to help you move quickly in the event you want to buy a foreclosed property at auction. How quick can they get you to the closing table if you buy a property at an absolute auction? Find out how the lender normally handles client applications, specifically yours, when you need them to move fast.

Finding the Best Property at the Best Price without Using Your Cash

When you meet with your banker, ask about lending options. Ask your lending officer to talk to you about the best ways to finance real estate purchases. See if they can offer new suggestions you may not know about. Many times, new products come out in lending packages with lower down payments required and other advantages you may be interested in. If you ask your loan officer to describe different financing packages to you, ideas may come into mind as you need them.

Some of the best financing options you may have will later involve a lender and a combination of lender- and seller-financing. You never know when the information you gather will come in handy when you are ready to make an offer. You will know what you can afford to do and seal the deal in writing.

There are going to be some properties that appeal to you far more than others. In theory, there may not be much difference in the properties when you compare them. However, if you find one property will be easier to finance than the other, then that property will clearly be the one to buy. You want to buy from sellers who *really* want to sell to you. How do you find those sellers? You have to learn to go where most speculators will not go. This may mean you dabble in real estate holdings in less desired areas of town. After all, it is these areas where foreclosures are common.

You can find investors or sellers willing to sell to you but you may have to search them out if you want to buy on your terms. You will find financing from investors and sellers who will want to finance you under your terms and conditions. Many of these people will not have a choice because the bank is ready to foreclose.

For the investor who wants to accumulate several properties in a short time or for the investor who recognizes the financial need for creative financing, certain properties will have more appeal than others. As you are beginning to accumulate properties, the best thing you can do is to find the properties that would take as little money out of your pocket as possible. Look for creative financing, owner financing, lease options, subject-to deals, and rent-to-own contracts. Watch the newspaper for advertisements so you can recognize a deal when you see one.

If you want to play with the big boys who invest in lots of real estate, creative financing is a tool to use.

The Paper Trail You Need to Prepare

Investors need a good record keeping system. How you keep your records is entirely up to you but you must have them; otherwise when tax season rolls around each year, you will be running for the hills to avoid the IRS.

Find an area in your home where you will keep all your real estate closing documents, invoices for repairs, homeowners insurance, and other important documents. Make a folder or individual file for each property you own so you are able to keep each one completely separate.

Keep all receipts separated as well. Following are some things you need to keep for each of your properties:

- Keep track of all **repairs** done on the property whether they are true repairs or improvements. Keep your receipts from Home Depot or your local hardware store, keep your bill from the electrician, save your paint store receipts. Just keep it all!

- Hold on to the receipts when you pay your **insurance** premiums.

- Save your electric and water bill **receipts** if you are paying them.

- Anything regarding termite or home **inspections** should be placed with the home's information and receipts for the treatments.

- Save any **cleaning bills** such as home cleaning or carpet cleaning.

- Hold on to **lawn service bills**.

Make sure any kind of maintenance work or lawn service is minimized when possible. The more work you can do yourself on a fixer-upper, the more money you will have to put back into your other real estate holdings.

Keeping good records will not only help you at tax time; but it will also help you when you are deciding on the next property you want to buy. You will have the records you need to decide which properties have been most profitable to you and act accordingly.

Chapter Four

Living on Borrowed Dimes

Very few people start out in real estate investing without borrowing some money from someone. Unless you are fortunate enough to use family money to begin your investments, loans will become your lifeline, and managing them will be important to your success. If you do not learn to manage the loans, those loans will make it impossible for you to manage your real estate business effectively.

Before you begin negotiations with sellers or lenders, there are some things you should know about the lending side of investing. Financing your investments is something you will become familiar with, but you also need to know that closing costs are not cheap. In many seller-financed deals, a seller will pay a portion or all of them. In some cases, they will be greatly reduced because the seller and buyer agree to skip over some of the typical steps performed to close and transfer title. In seller financed properties, it is typical to see a closing without a survey, appraisal, or even a home inspection. All these are costly and can save you money initially. However, you need the information you obtain from these three steps. Therefore, you have to weigh what you give up for those lower closing costs.

FOOD FOR THOUGHT

A young couple decides to take their $5,000 and find a home to call their own. They check out their options through a local real estate agent and find the home of their dreams. After they secure the financing, they begin to plan. They are excited beyond anyone's wildest imagination—until they get a call from their lender.

The lender calls to let the couple know about their closing costs. The couple is shocked to learn a few hundred dollars will not do the trick. The voice on the phone is apologetic as he explains he forgot to mention the closing costs and just assumed the buyer would know about them.

The deal is dead before the lender hangs up because when the couple told the agent they had $5,000 to spend, they meant they had no more than $5,000. Deals die hard because people are not educated on the cost of lending and do not realize how expensive it is to close a transaction on a house.

Loans and Fees

It is quite costly to secure a loan from a lender. Above the interest you pay for using the funds, the bank charges fees to secure the loan. It is the cost of doing business with a lender. Following, are some of the fees you should expect to pay when closing a loan through a traditional lender:

1. Loan Origination Fees such as application and processing fees

2. Fee for pulling the credit report

3. Courier Fees

4. Survey and Appraisals

5. Title Insurance

6. Title Search

7. Recording Fees

The above suggestions are often overlooked when a new investor starts out, and they can add up shockingly fast. Many agents I know tell their clients up front to count on 3 percent of the sales price for closing fees. While I have found that to be on the high side in many cases, it is better to be safe than sorry, and when you start shopping for properties it is best to have more than enough cash on hand to complete the deal.

Creatively financing your real estate investments is NOT a get-rich-quick scheme. In fact, be prepared to dedicate some time and effort to working as a real estate investor. You can own several properties and yet fall short of "rich" unless you know how to invest in income producing properties that will appreciate in value and provide a good cash flow.

Hard Truths

Even though we are looking at creatively financing real estate investments, you need to know it will be important for you to become a skilled money manager. Even though you will be buying and selling property more on credit than cash, you still need to be able to manage the properties you are buying. You should also become aware of how you use your credit. If you learn to manage your credit effectively, you can use it more appropriately in your speculation activities.

Example One: Positive Cash Flow/Sound Investment

Jane and Tom purchase a home for $50,000. Through a purchase-money mortgage, they pay $1,000 down and finance the balance over 15 years at 6.9 percent interest and they have a payment of $437.69. They rent the home for $565 per month and realize a positive cash flow on the property of $127.31 per month. Do you think this is a good investment? Yes, indeed. Now, even though they are not really making $127.31 because of taxes and insurance, they are still covering their payment and there is enough left over to cover their homeowners insurance.

Example Two: No Cash Flow/Sound Investment

Jane and Tom purchase a lake lot for $100,000 and realize a payment of $658.60 per month. They were able to purchase by putting up their home for collateral. They do not have a down payment invested in the property. In two years, the lake front lot is in high demand because all the other lake front lots have sold. They sell their property for $145,000 at the end of the 24th month of ownership. They have paid 24 payments of $658.60 and have $15,806.40 invested in the lot. A profit of $29,193.60 is realized. Even though the cash flow was not there, the property appreciated in value and the investment was solid.

Example Three: Cash Flow/Poor Investment

Jane and Tom buy a beachfront condo for $150,000 and put $10,000 down on the property. Amortized over 30 years, their payments are $922.04 with a 6.9 percent interest rate. The property rents during the summer months by the week at $1,000 week but the area is seasonal. At the end of the first season, the couple has rented the condo for a total of eight weeks and with the area deserted, that is the only cash flow they will receive on the condo. With maintenance fees of $200 a month, the condo is a poor investment if based on cash flow alone. However, if the couple hangs onto the condo, it should appreciate. Still, by all reasonable investment standards, the condo is considered a poor investment.

Part of your money management will begin with learning how to ride out the volatile markets. There will be times in real estate when the market turns. For example, you will see a strong indication of a buyer's market when the economy takes a dive. Learning to muddle through these difficult times means holding on to what you have while planning for what you intend to buy. A failing economy means buying opportunities. When you can capitalize on these opportunities, generally you can profit.

In addition to knowing how to stay afloat during tough markets, real estate investors should do the following:

- Never put all your money in one place. You may discover you have a knack for handy-man specials but find that an apartment building with long-term tenants can pay your bills. Diversify and keep all your options open.

- Always deal with several banks, never just one. Sure the FDIC has your money insured but you do not want anyone to know all your financial business. Usually banks offer different lending packages so that one bank is more attractive than another.

- Have a bankroll to help you manage your real estate portfolio within your means and manage it like a budget.

- Keep cash on hand or at least within easy access. Do not have all your cash tied up to the point that you cannot touch it within a few hours. Sure you want as much of it as possible hard at work for you but you should not have all of it at work at one time. Otherwise you are not going to be able to cover yourself quickly in a crisis.

Take the opportunity to learn from other investors. Many of the old timers who have been in the business of buying and selling real properties understand what it takes to be successful. See what you can learn from them.

The Change Up and Breaking a Million

When a volatile market takes a hard swing to the other side of the spectrum, it is called a switch. In this business, the switch can surprise an investor. If an investor is not prepared to hold what he owns, a turn around in the market can mean losses. For example, if you are an investor who likes to buy properties and flip them, a volatile market could catch you off guard. If you buy a bit too high as the economy begins to decline and cannot be content to hold onto what you have, you will sell at a loss.

Market movements can hurt even those people with large bank accounts and endless assets. Even with several pieces of real estate in your investment portfolio, if you start selling when you should be buying and buying when you should be selling, you are caught up in what is known as a switch and you can lose money. Playing the volatile market back and forth is costly.

For investors who play most of their money when the market is most volatile, it is not uncommon to become a desperate player, meaning they are investing money they cannot afford to lose and they are bound to lose. This is why: if you cannot hang on to what you have when the market is moving one way and then another too swiftly to determine which way it is going, you need to *sit on* your properties. Scared money always loses in investments. There are times when you should just hold and if you are doing anything other than playing the waiting game, you also run the risk of loss.

When volatile markets happen, winners are set apart from losers. A winner can turn a volatile market into one that works in his or her favor but that is because he or she can afford it. Losers cannot. Winners, typically the old pros in the real estate industry, will watch for the right buying opportunities and selling opportunities and will not get in any hurry to do either. If they need to sell in a hot buyer's market, they will creatively finance their properties to another buyer making it easier for them to move it.

When you are buying and selling as a real estate investor, you need to become educated by talking with your agent and listening to housing market analysts. When you buy a property, think about what the best and worst case scenarios will be for you when you buy and do the same thing again when you are selling. Think about what will happen if you just hold it. Will it appreciate?

Even though earlier in the book we talked about working with agents and allowing them to understand your needs, we also want to add something else in here for you to consider. In volatile markets, unless you have a good relationship with your real estate agent and they understand exactly how you like to buy and sell, you will have to watch for them to make a mistake when the market turns.

During this time, you often have to keep him at arm's length because they are just as human as you are. They may expect a quick recovery or bounce back if the market is low when it may be ready for a further descent.

Remember, a real estate agent only makes a commission on a sale that closes. They are paid to be optimistic about the market. It is their job. In volatile markets, it is important to talk openly with your agent but never give away too much information because you do not know for sure if they have your best interests in mind until you work with them for awhile.

Be careful about going in with the top dollar you are willing to pay for anything especially when the market is volatile and do not let your agent know right off the bat what you are willing to pay. I know doing this might appear to be deceptive, but remember their commission is their livelihood and slip-ups can cost you money. In volatile markets, the slip ups *will cost you* money. The best approach to take with your seller or your agent (when they are working with your seller), is that you are always offering your best price. Whether you are buying or selling counter with the "best you are willing to do."

In sales, this is known as one hand on the doorknob. In other words, make your offer and then look as if it is your final offer. In all your real estate transactions, always look as if the door could slam on the offer you are making and you could not care less. This way, when the seller looks at what you are proposing, they give it some serious thought and if they cannot do it, they will come back with their best counter offer. In volatile markets, that's what you want.

In a changing market, the speculators who are able to keep their heads above water are usually the people who can come out on top. However, if you are a speculator who has a world of investments out there financed through your original sellers, you will need to plan ahead so volatility does not end the start of a prosperous career.

Many people will begin their real estate speculating career on borrowed money. If you do, you have to be able to ride out the market when it is not always favorable. That is why it is so important to either have a bankroll to do it, a banker behind you who can be your financier, or some other Plan B!

Anonymous investor from Sevier County, Tennessee

No one knows what my bottom dollar is when negotiating. I will not even tell my wife because she might tell her best friend. I want my real estate agent to be in the dark about my finances because she may know the agent on the other side of the deal. When I was a young man, I found this out the hard way. I told my agent everything I knew. Before long, I realized the agent spilled everything I told her. She would tell what she thought I would pay, and it dawned on me after dealing with her that I was paying the price I told her I would pay. So I just shut up.

Chapter Five

Negotiating with Sellers to Get the Financing You Need

S mart investors know that to buy properties using creative financing, they need to learn the art of negotiation—not easy if your credit is in dire-straights, but if you take the time to talk to your sellers, you will discover it is easy to finance your purchases with the help of a willing seller.

In real estate investing, you have to be prepared to make a quick move when dealing with sellers of hot properties. The capitalist who moves first is the first to profit. Investors who are able to make quick decisions and stand by them eager to develop those decisions into profits are the administrators getting things done. They know the market is not going to wait on them to make up their mind on something and an anxious seller will not either.

As an investor, you have to be able to make a quick decision and feel good about it; therefore, become educated in real estate and know the markets where you invest. By doing your research, you will not second-guess yourself when opportunities find you or when you find them; you just act and you know you are safe in your actions. This is where good negotiations with a seller really are an asset.

Seller on the Fly and Investor on the Run

The time it takes to negotiate with sellers can be a friend or an enemy. For this reason, be prepared with your best approach to take with sellers for financing. Take the time to learn the art of negotiating a good real estate deal that will require some seller financing or creative moves by the seller. To do this, you should understand there will be times when it will not be advantageous to work with the seller, but if you feel that you are making a deal with a credit monster, find your credit somewhere else.

Most people do believe the only people who use creative measures to finance their home or other real estate purchases are credit morons capable only of bumming credit to secure their real estate deals. Locating investors is hardly the same thing. Other than your seller, you can find private lenders willing to look at your investment opportunity. Financiers search for investors who are safe bets because of their investment. Real estate entrepreneurs who are eager to finance outside the realm of traditional lending are a tool for capitalists to gain more profits. When they have a keen interest in a property, and they take the position as the money bags behind the deal, it is generally a safe transaction as far as they are concerned. It is also more appealing when the private lender is taking back the position of equity sharing. A person or group of investors who hold the purse strings are ultimately in control and should the buyer default, they are protected because they have an investment secured by the real estate itself.

Selling Your Ideas to the Seller

A seller who is financially capable of carrying the paper for a buyer is usually willing to enter a purchase-money mortgage agreement, which is nothing more than a mortgage agreement between buyer and seller in which the seller is financing the transaction. If you are working with a real estate agent who is keeping your overall goals and interests in mind, you should have no problem negotiating with flexible sellers. Your agent should have handled the preliminary work for you and should be bringing you properties you can afford to buy either with cash or through creative financing.

Often, sellers who want to finance their properties will advertise a property for sale with owner financing available. They may advertise they are willing to lease-purchase, or they may even advertise the property outright as owner financing. If the agent who is handling all your real estate transactions does his or her homework, you will likely only meet with sellers who are at least open to some creative financing that will help you meet your investment goals.

The advantage to working with a real estate agent with access to the multiple listing service is finding hot sellers—homes and other properties that sell quickly because of price or a flexible seller. If an agent is watching new listings daily, he or she will see the hot sellers and let you know as soon as there is a new listing that you may be interested in seeing.

Often, you will need to create your own opportunities on the properties you are interested in pursuing. If you learn how to talk to your sellers about creatively financed deals, you may be surprised by how many great deals you can land with creative financing. The potential is unlimited.

You want to show the seller who may not have thought about creatively financing their property what is in it for them — more money. You want to mention the tax advantages they may find in seller-financing and, finally, remind them of how quickly a deal can reach the closing table when a purchase-money mortgage is used. If you know the house would never be appraised for the price the seller is asking (but you still want it anyway), have your realtor mention this to the seller's real estate agent. It is something you can use later, but let the seller's realtor introduce the fact that the property will never be appraised for the selling price. In that case, the best options for a seller are to sell the property on a purchase-money mortgage or find a cash buyer. After all, a traditional lender will expect the money they loan on real estate to be secured by property which appraises for the loan amount.

Working with a seller who has the financial ability to carry the mortgage can be advantageous to you, but never lose sight of the fact you need to assure the seller it is most advantageous to him. When you meet with the seller or when your real estate agent meets with the seller or his agent, be sure everyone understands the profit potential. It is best to attach a worksheet or an amortization schedule so the seller can see the money he will make. Saying it and seeing it can be quite different. Show your seller the purchase price and then show him the amount of money he will make on interest.

Simply going in with an offer to purchase with a brief coverage of the money will not be that beneficial to you. If you are buying a house for $70,000 and are trying to convince the seller to carry the money for you for 15 years at the interest rate of 7 percent so you can keep your payment around $790, the $790 figure could be all the seller comprehends. However, if you go into the negotiations with the $70,000 and you explain the interest rate you are willing to pay is 7 percent and at the end of 15 years the seller will have made an additional $73,500 that sounds a lot better. Moreover, if you learn how to amortize the mortgage over 15 years with a balloon payment in five years or so, your deal is attractive to a seller. They make more money on their home and they are not tied down to carry your mortgage for 15 long years.

Do not approach a seller with the idea that he will be the keeper of your mortgage for the next 10–15 years. Experience will prove to you over and over again when you are on either side of the closing table, five to seven years is about it for a real estate financing relationship besides traditional lending. In many cases, a seller finds three to five years is enough and they are typically ready to grab their cash and move on to another deal. Keep this in mind as you begin to invest in properties where you want the seller to finance or help out with creative ways for you to buy their property.

Another point worth mentioning here is if you have good credit and you have a seller who is adamant about seeing it, let them sneak a peek. What do you have to lose? I would not recommend giving them a copy of it, but if you need to flash it, do so.

Writing Winning Offers

If you want sellers to finance you, learn to write offers to purchase that will appeal to them. If you have a real estate agent who is interested in closing deals, he or she will advise you on certain aspects of writing winning offers to purchase. Avoid asking for trivial things such as a carpet allowance or for a ceiling fan to remain that the seller already denied you. If you are going to ask for seller financing or for the seller to help with some creative aspects to the financing, avoid antagonizing them.

When writing a winning offer to purchase, keep the following in mind:

- What is the house worth?

- What do you want to pay for the house?

- What will you pay for the house?

- Ideally, how do you want to finance your purchase?

- Do you have a plan B if your ideal situation falls through?

- What items must stay with the home for you to buy the property?

- Are you willing to forgo these items if the seller is not willing to leave them?

A winning offer to purchase will make the difference in whether you are able to secure a signature from the seller. If you are writing an offer on a piece of property or a home that your real estate agent has told you will sell fast, do not play games; get down to business and write up your best offer first. You may not have the opportunity to receive a counter offer if the seller receives several offers at one time on the property.

Let's Talk Money

Before you contemplate writing an offer to purchase, you should consider whether you are going to be able to secure the financing you need if your contract for purchase is accepted by the seller. In that case, you want to be able to secure the note quickly before the contract is expected to be executed. This is something you will need to pay attention to when you are writing your offers for purchase. The contract for purchase will have an area committed to designating an intended closing date. Take pains to set the closing date out further than you anticipate it arriving. In most cases, in the offer to purchase, the contract will state on or before a certain date, and the seller will be hoping for the "before" rather than the date specified.

It is important to take pains to read each increment of an agent's sales contract or offer for purchase and you need to understand if you do not close on or before a certain date, a seller has the right to sell to someone else and keep your retainer in most circumstances. This is why it is so important to know what you are signing before you sign it and to know the best way to write your contracts for purchase. You want to be sure you have described the financing you are hoping to secure and if you are planning to secure outside financing through a traditional lender or through outside creative measures, make sure you know you can obtain the financing. Ideally, before you write an offer to purchase or sign the binder check, you will already know you can afford it and how you are going to pay for it.

When you begin your search for creative means to finance your purchase, keep the following in mind:

- Seller financing

- Second Mortgages

- Assumable Mortgages

- Private Lenders

- Equity Sharing

- Overlapping Mortgages

- Wraparound Mortgages

- Lease Options and Rent-to-own

- Options

All the above mortgages and ideas are good to use in financing your investment properties. Take the time to learn as much as you can about each individual mortgage and find out what you need to know before you make an offer to purchase. You never know when you may be using any one of the above suggestions to finance your real estate transaction creatively.

Looking at Your Options

When you find a property you like, take a moment to look at several options. Work it out on paper. Before writing an offer to purchase, take a look at the best way to finance *this* real estate purchase. You will want to look at different ways to finance each individual property you buy because no two properties will be financed the same way. This is one reason you need to get to know a mortgage loan officer and bankers in your area so you can be familiar with traditional loan packages. You will also want to consider the options we discuss so you are familiar with them before you begin.

You will probably not finance all your properties the same way. One key factor to remember whenever you negotiate with your seller is the profit potential. Negotiate with every seller who works with you in a way that enables them to recognize the benefits to them. If you are able to familiarize yourself with all aspects of creative financing, you will be able to write winning offers to purchase with creative financing as the focus and close deals that work best for you while ensuring that the seller feels really good about the transaction.

Take a moment to consider the advantages of adding the property to your investment portfolio and choosing your financing package. What will you gain by owning the property? The goal is to make a profit. Will you realize one? Will the way you choose to finance your purchase enable you to profit much sooner?

Chapter Six

Using the Investor's Money and Credit

An investor starting out in the real estate business may be surprised to find out that one way of getting financing is with the help of another investor. It is common for first-time home buyers or home buyers with bad or no credit to turn to the resources of a private investor or for investors to use each other for financing even if they have excellent credit.

Approach a private investor with confidence. The private investor is someone who wants to invest in properties especially if he or she can find another investor who appears to have his or her investment dollars going in the right place — real estate. You want to look for an investor who is knowledgeable about the business and not just stepping into the role of financial backer. The more the private investor knows, the better because he or she will be somewhat open to more creative financing measures and often can devise an innovative package for you.

Trump the Contrarian

I like watching Donald Trump. He is arrogant, smooth, and all business. When it comes to real estate, no one buys or sells bigger or better. He knows how to work a great deal. He is not only the man behind one of the largest real estate fortunes but he is also the guru who has put together some remarkable deals.

Donald Trump means business when it comes to buying and selling real estate. If anyone knows how to work a stimulating and almost artistic transaction, it is Trump. His methods have been contrarian-like and he has proven he can go where others will not go and still make a fortune. In doing so, he has become one of the most powerful players in real estate today.

An investor who is keen on finding creative ways to finance their real estate investments can take a lesson from Trump, the king of real estate creativity. He has been able to obtain funding for some of the most elaborate projects in the world. He has found investors for projects most people would never consider but he has proven he is a champ in the business. His deals are solid, profitable, and — best of all — the way Trump likes them to put him in the public eye.

As a real estate speculator you will not be operating at the level of Donald Trump. (At least not at first!) However, you must comprehend the risks involved when using outsiders to help with financing investment properties, particularly when there are shared-equities involved. When you are financially supported in your endeavors by a person who is to share in the equity realized from the property, often your profit is so limited it is not worth the trouble to involve a private lender. This is when you may want to consider another avenue.

Be wary of a partnership with a buy-sell arrangement. If you are in over your head with business people who have more money than you do, you most definitely want to use caution when working out terms on big deals. Buy-sell contracts are never a good arrangement when you are in partnerships with far wealthier individuals. It is too risky. However, despite the risks involved anytime you deal with a second or third party for backing, private lending can offer you the flexibility to obtain the precise financing you need to make a profit in the end.

Stability is the reason a private lender chooses to back people in their real estate acquisitions. The reason it is considered stable is because history shows real estate has been a good investment even in the worst economies. Is it because it is such a sound investment or is it because the players, especially the big player, in the industry have proven they know how to manage their holdings? Possibly.

Still, when a private lender or a seller goes in to help finance a purchase for another speculator, he is not dealing with a large whale in the real estate pond. Typically, he is dealing with the ordinary guy next door and yet, he still feels compelled to do it believing his investment is safe. Why? Because it is.

While the risks involved with real property purchases generally fall back on the person holding the deed of trust, the property does stand good for the loan obtained most of the time. Unless the financier loans more on the property than the real estate's value, which would not be considered a smart business move, the house or land should stand good for the note while appreciating in value.

When you begin to look at the methods of a contrarian-type investor, you will see this type of investor is the person who will want to creatively finance the properties he or she buys and sells.

He knows he is in a good business and he will be able to find people who want to sell to him based on these principles while he will never be short on finding someone to unload the properties he buys in the same manner. How does he know this? Because he is going against the norm and when the contrarian finds a way to go against the masses with a strong investment tool such as real estate, the results can be favorable.

Another thing the contrarian investor realizes is that not everyone is going to have the 5 to 20 percent down payment and since not everyone will have what the more popular lenders will need, a contrarian investor can use that to his or her advantage. There is a need for what he or she will be able to provide when selling. When he buys, by buying on creative terms, he enables himself some flexibility to accumulate more properties in the areas where he wants to buy. At the same time, he still looks pretty good on paper should he need to see a lender for a particular short-term play.

As an investor whose goals are to cash in on the large demand for real estate, recognizing the demand alone is not enough. As a contrarian, you will find ways to invest in real estate using creative financing going against the ordinary methods of an investor who finds his funding from a traditional lender.

When "The Donald" wants to finance a property, he looks at all his options. When he moves to attach financing for his projects, he can put together a financing package that sings with appeal. He will do things others will not do while developing areas others would never dream of developing. If in doubt, look at what he did in New York with the West Side. If anyone has proven a contrarian can play with the big boys, and even become the largest, it is Trump. What lender or private financier would not get behind him?

A financier who knows real estate will always be in demand and that if the right investment comes along, it only makes sense for to team up with an investor. Capitalists realize they must find ways to finance real estate projects creatively for others to make a win-win situation for all parties involved. This is how financing real estate creatively can become a wining situation because it creates more opportunities for the real estate investor looking to buy and also for the financial backer who is ready to offer his or her assistance — as well as collecting interest money from a capable investor.

Even with the demand for real estate going up, there are still good times to buy and more appropriate times to sell, something the contrarian-investor has learned. A contrarian does typically go against what everyone else is doing, but he does not do it if it is not going to be profitable just for the sake of going against what everyone is doing at the time. He knows and recognizes there will be certain times to buy and better times to sell than others. This is particularly important because the investor who has the ability to know what to do and when to do it using the market trends will be successful by the way he or she meticulously chooses and then finances the properties he or she buys.

Buck the System

In many areas of the country, you will often find real estate better than in other areas. Often, the locations to buy are those areas where the market appears to be slow. Even better, if you can find an area where lenders are really tight with their loan approvals, you can buck the system by doing a number of things:

- Creatively finance without traditional lenders

- Use a subject-to deals which are discussed later

- Use creative financing methods as a vehicle to purchase more property while holding it and waiting for the appropriate time to sell

There is a season for everything, even buying real estate. If you look for the right time to buy and the right financing when you buy, you will not pay too much for the property. Instead you are essentially acquiring the land or home on your own terms with the end result of profit in mind. Often, an investor will even buy a little high using a purchase money mortgage or a lease-option because he has already planned how he will profit from the purchase. While it is never advisable to buy high, there will be times when buying high will be warranted if you already know where and how you will be able to turn the purchase into a profit.

Will That Be Cash or Credit?

An outside investor is always interested in finding opportunities to work with other real estate investors. They feel that their investment is secure, and they can count on the cash flow from the investor they finance in most cases. Predictably, there are investors who are not the best business partners so take the time to know your financial backer.

Investors use various methods to finance another investor. They can use cash, of course, or they can use their credit. They can be pretty creative in how they find the money to finance another party and will use various loan packages to get the deal done if needed.

FOOD FOR THOUGHT FROM AN OLD TIMER IN REAL ESTATE

Let me give you some examples of why I invest

There is an IPO to watch on the stock market and it is supposed to be the best initial public offering in a decade. A man sells some of his blue-chip stocks and hopes for the best as he dumps thousands of dollars in the IPO stock. After a couple of days, he has lost $2,000, and since it did not double within days as initially expected, he sells it. Two weeks later, the stock is climbing and analysts are watching closely with high expectations.

An investor buys Coca-Cola stock at an unbelievably low price of $15 per share and as analysts advise against the stock, the investor's large holding in the company skyrockets. Today Warren Buffet begins to give away billions of dollars, and some remember a time when he dared to do what others would not.

An old man lies dying on his bed while his children gather around him. They are sad to see their father go. They adore him. However, as they treasure their last moments with their father, he lies in sorrow with a heart full of regret. As a young man, this gentleman watched as his friends bought and sold real estate but he never had the stomach for it. Avoiding the risk was safe and comfortable. Now he leaves behind only enough money for his children to bury him.

Down the street in an attorney's office, a young couple meets with another seller to close on their fifth apartment complex. They are investors and by the time they reach the age of 35, they will be considered real estate millionaires. They have

FOOD FOR THOUGHT CONTINUED

made wise investments since they started their lives together. They are building a future for themselves and for the children they will someday leave behind.

Why do you think so many people are content with what they have and settle for less when they could build wealth? Why are individuals content to live a normal, average life when with a little effort and risk, they could accumulate so much more? Many would-be investors wonder what it takes to be a success, but they ignore the signs right in front of them. They choose to look the other way when an income producing opportunity falls in their lap. They do not know how to get an investment venture going because they have no means, according to them, to purchase real estate or stocks. They even refuse to believe that they know how. My friends, I just believe these are the people who are too content *with not knowing* how. Today, there are too many opportunities for investments to be financed. Playing dumb does not work anymore. You have to want to learn how, but if you have no ambition, I cannot help you, and this book cannot help you. You are your own worst enemy because you simply will not try.

Anonymous Contributor

The biggest concern in investor-investor agreements comes down to the money, of course. Investors who are the financiers of properties will want a higher interest rate than the prime rate. Typically, they will not give you a discount because there is nothing in it for them if they does. The investor-buyer who is looking for a financial backer cannot make any money dealing with another investor who is too focused on big profits from one deal. It can become a tug of war for potential profits.

A seller who finances his buyer will generally be content to make money from the sale of the house while the private lender will focus more on the profit he will make by allowing the buyer to use his money. The homeowner will look at how much more money is in it for them when they seller-finance; whereas the private lender will look more at just the interest rate unless he or she is also interested in equity sharing.

Your job as a buyer is to find people who can work with you and offer you the most attractive terms. Who will that be? It will be the one who is offering those terms to you now that you recognize will benefit you greatly later.

Approaching Creditworthy Investors

After you find the investors you need to finance your real estate transaction, you need to talk to them about your goals. You should first establish the fact that you are both going to trust one another and this can be done with an air-tight contract through a real estate attorney. Sorry, but the good old hand shake does not do the trick anymore.

After you establish verbal terms, write it up and put a pen to it as quickly as possible. As a buyer remember often a private investor does make his money from the deals he repossesses. With that in mind, make sure you are able to meet your payments and hold up your end of the deals you make.

Finding the Best Investors

In some cases, the best chance you have to secure financing for a home is through an investor and often the only investor who will take a chance on you will be a family member or close friend. The baby boomers needed outside help to finance their properties, and Generation X has been one financial catastrophe after another as we noted earlier.

If you are speculating and someone brings it to your attention that they are most interested in equity sharing, then you want to keep it simple. Take a look:

1. Bob wants to buy a handyman special but has no credit to finance a new home purchase so he approaches his parents.

2. Bob's parents agree to help him with his financing but want to be partners in the home purchase. They will use their money and credit to buy the home but they want to be equal partners when the house sells.

3. When Bob's house sells, his parents will get back their original investment if they paid cash and Bob will be paid for any improvements he made to the home.

4. Bob and his parents will split the profit.

There are some provisions which are made in equity-sharing arrangements. Make sure you understand what those might be. Generally, you have to decide who is going to be responsible for paying for minor improvements and how the person will be compensated for their time and supplies. Will this be settled once the property sells or as updates and repairs are completed?

Things to Know About Using Investors

An investor is all about the money when he or she steps into your real estate deal. The investor may be a friendly person and well spoken but when it comes down to the dollar, he will make sure he gets it!

Never forget who you are dealing with when you go outside the normal parameters of traditional lending. When you allow a private investor in, you are dealing with a real estate loan shark—not always, but often. While these investors may have put trust in the fact you will make timely payments, most could not care less if you do. After all, their investment is secure and if you do not pay them, they'll take the property.

The Investor-Investor Contract

When writing up an offer to buy real estate, I always encouraged clients to look out for their own best interests and when dealing with a contract between investors, the same holds true. If you are going to be working with an investor, you need to find one and quickly find an attorney to draw up an air-tight contract between the two of you, urging the attorney to keep your best interests in mind.

Ideally, if you are going to work with a private lender, you will find one in your local area with a good reputation. Should you be unable to find one on your own, ask around. Even though they are everywhere, they often wait in the shadows for the right opportunity. If you put the word out in the field that you are looking, one will show his or her face and help you out. They really have nothing to lose and much real estate to gain.

Chapter Seven

Options Are Gold

I f you want to make money using someone else's equity in their property and you are willing to gamble a little bit, options are the way to go. We are not talking about lease-options; we are talking about a more profitable way of doing business in real estate. In fact, if you are savvy about the real estate market, your risk will be minimal and the return on your initial investment will be great.

Many people use options to buy time. However, if you get into the habit of using options to buy time rather than just for profit, you will quickly discover options can be an expensive way to buy time unless you are exercising your option to buy.

Understanding Options

Understanding options is not all that difficult if you just keep things as simple as possible. For a better understanding, take a look at the following scenario:

FOOD FOR THOUGHT

Hal is a college student at a university close to his home. He has no money of his own so he lives at home and commutes to school. In a business class he learns about a seminar for real estate investments, and he attends it. He learns about options and decides to give them a whirl since he does not have income opportunities.

He borrows $3,000 from his parents and goes to work finding properties that are undervalued by their market price. He watches the local newspaper for the homes listed for sale by owner and calls property owners with an investment opportunity.

Finally, he locates his first seller who qualifies for an option contract. The house is on the market For Sale By Owner at $55,000 and after researching the property, Hal finds that with some minor updates it should bring about $80,000. In this case, Hal offers the seller the opportunity to make his $55,000 plus a few thousand more. He offers the seller a $250 option and offers to fix up the property. When it sells, they will split the difference. This particular option carries no deadline because Hal is going to put some money into improvements and more importantly, he is going to put his own labor into the project.

A few months later, the house is attractive. It sells for $82,000 and the original owner gets his $55,000, and Hal and the homeowner split the additional $27,000 for a total of $13,500 each. Hal put $250 into the option originally and an additional $1,800 in improvements but he still cleared $11,450 on his investment. Not bad for a college kid looking to invest in real estate.

Options can work a variety of different ways. There are several points to remember when choosing properties for options. The following list will help you:

- Choose undervalued properties. Decide on properties you know are priced below what the market would allow for the location and property.

- Be fair in what you offer potential partners in your options. Remember, you need them more than they need you.

- Be fair to yourself, too. In most cases options have deadlines. However, if you decide to work out an option on a property which is damaged or in need of repairs, be fair to yourself. If you are going to put some time and energy into the property, consider an open-ended contract until the property sells. Otherwise, you are out your money invested in the option and out the money you sank into the property on repairs, not to mention your time.

The Best Way to Use Options

Options are a great way to enter the world of real estate, but they are not ideal in every situation. For instance, if you are buying a home for yourself and plan to live in it, a lease-option is a better choice.

The reason for using options is for profit. Many investors would argue that it is one easy way to make good money without much of your own money invested. You can take out an option for $200 (or as little as a dollar) and then turn around and exercise your option and place thousands in your pocket overnight. It really is as simple as it sounds.

Approaching the Right Seller with an Option

I talked to several investors to get a better feel of the way they approach sellers about an option. One investor was open to sharing his information and his "option tactics" with me. His approach is in the following:

FOOD FOR THOUGHT

Joe told me, "Not everyone uses options the way I use them. I set out to find the properties in the worst possible shape and with the help of my agent; I convince the seller they will make more money if they choose to deal with me on an option." He also looks for vacant houses. Joe said he feels as if he has a better shot with another investor or property owner who has a house sitting vacant than if he tries to convince a seller to give him an option on the seller's current residence. "I am not infringing on anyone's privacy if I ask for an option on a fixer-upper."

His secret to approaching sellers with options is in his organizational skills as much as the way he presents his ideas to the seller. He lets the seller know what he is going to do to the home should the seller grant him an option and he lets the seller know he will take full responsibility for repairs and costs. However, in his option agreement, he points out; there is no deadline. After he steps in to work on the project, he feels he owns as much of the house as the original seller, and his contracts are air-tight.

Things to Know about Options

If you are going to work within the confines of options, you have to protect your interests. No one else will do it for you and if you are going to work on options and fixer-uppers, never agree to a deadline. If you do have a deadline, have an air-tight contract

Kay White
kwhite5048@earthlink.net
www.tricitiesarearealestate.com

Most people don't know about options and if they do, they do not understand them. If people just understood what an option is and how much money they can make using them, I believe more people would find a way to invest using options. In fact, I am sure of it because there is money to be made with options and who does not like making money?

so that the work you do on the project reverts back to a work-for-hire situation where you are reimbursed for your expenses and labor. When you get into option contracts, remember you are looking for the big money, and being paid for your updates and home improvements is not what you have in mind.

Years ago, options were used with less frequency than they are today. Today, an option is used as an investor's tool for financing his or her investments outside traditional investing. If used appropriately, options can enable you to accumulate more property, and best of all you can buy and sell on options and never have much of your own capital tied up in any one property.

A great resource for learning more about real estate options is *The Complete Guide to Real Estate Options: What Smart Investors Need to Know — Explained Simply*, available from Atlantic Publishing (**www.atlantic-pub.com**, Item # CGR-01). The book shows you how to control a vast real estate portfolio without ever actually buying property.

The Best Option Contract

The best contract for options is one that is lenient with time; the more time you can get on an option contract, the better off you are. If you limit yourself to six weeks or three months, the option will run out before you know it and you will be left without the opportunity to turn your investment into profit. Remember when you approach a seller, the first thing to keep in mind is the end result: profit. With options, you can find a means to an end by using them wisely when you first begin to invest in real estate. Often, you can use options to gain the capital you need to begin buying properties you intend to hold for the long-term.

In addition to having an option with a great deal of flexibility in time, you also want to have one which allows you the greatest potential for profit. How do you know which options will offer you the most profit? You do your research. Before you take out any option, make sure you are going through homes magazines to ensure you are buying in an area considered to be a lucrative market. See what is selling. Retrieve information from the court house and make sure you always have accurate CMAs to ensure you are going into an area where it will pay you handsome profits to pursue the options you want.

In years past, the folks who used the options were not the folks who had money but were just the opposite. They wore cheap suits and were in desperate need of a manicure and yet they showed up at my closing table with maybe $100 in the option contract. When they exercised their option and sat down with me, the seller, and the new buyer, I would hand them a check that I felt sure was the most money they had ever seen. Now, I see millionaires who are working with options and they seem to understand how to use them for substantial profits. Maybe the guys in the cheap suits just caught on a lot faster than the rest of us. The rest of us were at the tailors.

Virginia Attorney

Chapter Eight

So You Want to Be a Landlord

The wealthiest person I have ever known was a landlord and real estate investor. He was the wealthiest and to this day, remains one of the most humble people I have ever known. He made millions in real estate and when he died, he left his children millions because of real estate. In fact, the second, third, and fourth wealthiest people I have known are real estate millionaires several times over. The really neat thing about these people was and continues to be the fact they were unimpressed with their wealth. These people made their millions in real estate proving that ordinary people can grow their wealth in real property.

Even though some of the wealthiest people in the world have made their living in real estate, children seldom say, "I want to be a landlord when I grow up." Remember, the landlords of today will become tomorrow's millionaires despite lack of education. These are the people who will hold the keys (literally) to financial freedom.

Finding the Best Rental Properties

Finding properties suitable to rent is not that difficult, but finding properties that will generate cash flow and enough rental income to float on its own is another story. You must take into account that you have to carry more insurance, take precautions to ensure the home is in safe order, and you will often have to be available for the tenant when you would prefer to be left alone. Many investors would like to avoid these aspects of being a landlord, and you can avoid them by placing your rentals with a good property management firm.

So the questions begin for the new investor, where do you find the best rental properties and how do you go about buying them? There are some things to keep in mind when you are buying properties for rent, and here is a list of suggestions to make your search for the perfect rental properties easier.

- **Find properties in excellent locations.**
  When buying an investment property to rent, remember that you are buying a home to rent to another person or family who will probably care about their location. If you are buying a home in the city to rent, pay attention to where the property is located relative to schools, shopping, and churches because people looking in the city want convenience. If you are buying in the country, make sure the location provides some conveniences, too. People who buy in the country like ponds, a barn, and plenty of room to roam but they still want to be able to dial 9-1-1 and have someone there for them quickly in an emergency.

- **Find affordable properties so you can offer affordable rents.**

Remember if you pay too much for a property, you will have to charge too much rent. Buy smart and you will be able to rent smart.

- **Look around at the neighborhood and decide if you would live there.**
  If you dislike area, do you think anyone else will like it?

- **Look at CMA and other factors so you know if property holds its value.**
  Know how well the properties in the area are holding their value. What is resale like in the area? Are people moving in and out of the area frequently? If it is a high rental area, is there fast turnover and if so, why?

- **Check the area for other rentals.**
  Are there more home owners or renters in the area and is this viewed as a positive or a negative based on the area?

- **Talk with other landlords in the area.**
  Before you buy, find out what kind of war stories other landlords are willing to share with you.

What You Should Know Before You Become a Landlord

We have established that being a landlord is a big responsibility, and there are some things to consider before you jump in with both feet. You have to be prepared and you have to be willing to screen your tenants without prejudice but still with some good measure of common sense.

FOOD FOR THOUGHT

A friend of mine rents out property on the lake. He told me, "As a landlord, you are not supposed to make judgments. Discrimination against anyone for any reason is prohibited if you are going to be a landlord. Still, if you have someone to show up in a van from the '60s to look at your $250,000 rental on the lake and a puff of marijuana follows the crowd to the front door, use good judgment and find a way to rent it to someone else who is not going to have problems obeying the law." I have to agree.

Turning a Tenant into a Buyer

Should you decide not to be a landlord; the next best thing to do is to become a landlord who is willing to owner-finance to a tenant who will take on the responsibility of home ownership. Turning a tenant into a buyer for the property they would be renting is of great advantage to the home owner because the investor will not be going out in the middle of the night to unclog a sink.

As an investor, when you own one of your rental properties free and clear, the best thing you can do for your tenant and really for yourself is to sit down and talk with your tenant about home ownership. Explain that you are interested in helping them become a home owner if they are interested in becoming one. Ideally, you will want to have a steady tenant for some time before you offer your renter this opportunity.

There are several ways you can approach this with your potential buyer/tenant. You can explain the concept of rent-to-own to them in which case the tenant will keep renting with a portion of their rent going towards the purchase of the property. You and

FOOD FOR THOUGHT

A tenant rents a home for five years. He makes his payment on the first day of the month and he has never been late. The only time he bothers the landlord is over things such as a water heater problem or on the occasion he locked himself out of the house. Otherwise, he has been a good tenant paying $500 a month.

The landlord decides to offer the tenant the opportunity to buy the home and the tenant takes him up on it. The rent of $500 a month remains the same in the form of a mortgage payment but the landlord's duties are over. The tenant is now a homeowner who must take care of his own water heater, and lock-outs are handled by the locksmith. Not a bad deal for the landlord who becomes the lender. He or she still sees timely payments without the headaches.

the tenant will go to an attorney's office and sign legal documents indicating how much of the rent will be applied toward ownership each month. At the end of the agreed period of time, you sign the deed over to the tenant and they own the property.

Some investors prefer to just owner finance the property to the tenant, in which case you would talk to the tenant about a 15- or 30-year term loan, agree upon the interest rate and see an attorney to close the deal. They would continue to make payments to you just as they did when they rented only they will be building equity in their own property because they would own the home from the closing date forward with you as their lender.

Turning a tenant into a homeowner can be rewarding; it can save you headaches and generally work out favorably for all parties involved. However, you must be prepared to foreclose should your buyer fail to pay you. When you go from being landlord to being lender, you must keep your financial interests in focus and remain steadfast in getting your money in and getting it on time.

Things to Know About the Renting Business

It used to drive me crazy. As a real estate agent, I remember talking to a couple of my investor-clients who felt really sorry for themselves because of the "headaches" their properties caused them. The worst one was an older guy who had never held a full-time job in his life because he was an investor with plenty of cash flowing into his bank accounts and wallet. Yet, to hear him speak, you would think he had no interest in real estate. It was just too difficult to make an income. Still, he would have me meet him at the golf course to sign contracts, and his tee times were always the focus of his day—not how soon he would be punching the time clock to go home.

Yes, investors do have it made. In my first book we discussed this briefly but now I want to elaborate because in my humble opinion, there is enough business to go around. Below are some facts about the lifestyle of the investor making wise investment decisions:

- They set their own hours.

- They can easily hire and afford a property management company to handle the labor.

- They vacation more than the rest of us.

- They never recommend it to keep the competition down.

- They call it a get-quick-rich scheme.

- They can sell out anytime if it is all that bad.

Real estate is the goose laying the golden eggs. Look at Trump and then take a look around at the investors who are straight-faced about how bad the market is as they hop in their fancy sports car and head to the golf course. Believe me, being a landlord is a cake walk compared to working 12-hour shifts in a hot manufacturing plant.

Contracts You Need Before You Become a Landlord

Many landlords keep all kinds of forms on hand. One thing to love about working with a property management firm: you can avoid keeping forms on hand and you do not have to handle the business end of contracts and deposits or collect rents and payments.

Still, if you are going to be a landlord who plans to handle the leasing end of the business alone, you should have all the legal forms. A word of caution to the self-operating landlord: do not settle for the forms on the Internet. Instead, see an attorney and be vested in your business with forms and contracts that are legal and binding should you ever need them to be so.

Chapter Nine

Finding Deals in Vacation Rentals, Foreclosures, and Subject-to Deals

Wise investors know there is a time to buy and a time to sell. You will often hear real estate agents and investors say, "It is a buyers' market" or "It is a sellers' market." What this means is that when it is a "buyers' market" there are too many properties on the market, and sellers will be more apt to settle on a reasonable price to move real estate. In a sellers' market, the opposite is true. There are not that many properties on the market in the area where the property is located, or the seller has something everyone wants. For example, a lakefront home in an exclusive 20-property lakefront community becomes available for sale. It is the first home in the subdivision to be offered for sale in five years. There are only five lakefront subdivisions in the whole town, and this subdivision is located closest to shopping. The sellers would be considered to be selling in a sellers' market.

At the same time, a beautiful estate is placed on the market when the interest rates are low and there are numerous properties and large estates in the same location. The seller would then be trying to sell his estate in a buyers' market. Smart buyers will use their knowledge of other properties on the market and comparative market analysis to pounce on the seller for a lower selling price if they truly want to buy the estate the seller is selling.

There are several really good times to buy. Following, you will see when market conditions determine it is a time to buy and why some other factors can prompt a buyer to buy quickly:

- If interest rates are low — it is a time to buy.

- If you are able to find a property before it goes into foreclosure, usually it is a time to buy.

- Foreclosures can move someone toward a purchase. If a foreclosure is in good shape — it is a time to buy.

- If there are too many properties on the market in the area — it is a time to buy.

- If a bank or mortgage company holds too many REO-owned properties — it is a time to buy.

As a real estate investor, learn about the stock market because it often affects the real estate market. For instance, the real estate market is affected in a "bear market." Profit margins expected from real estate sales typically decline in a bear market quicker than in a bullish market.

Intelligent investors subscribe to real estate reports and fall market reports. They will take note when one area of the country is suffering while other areas of the country thrive. They will ask questions and find out why. At the same time, they will know what affects their area of the housing market and act accordingly.

One of the reasons an investor will enlist the services of a licensed real estate agent is because he needs one. Just like a stock market investor enlists the services of a stock broker, the real estate investor knows experienced agents are often privy to insider information that may help them plan ahead.

A real estate agent can offer advice and help with a comparative market analysis (CMA) on the areas where you are interested in buying. As a contrarian, you have to be careful because what you learn from a real estate broker you will use to go against the norm and, if an agent recognizes this, the broker may feel that you are not listening. Let your agent know you value their input and then go ahead and reinvent your wheel.

In real estate, the only investors who succeed **in certain markets** are the contrarians. They are not afraid of the risk and are not intimidated when the Fed has something to say. These investors will survive in the market because they have no fear of it. They reinvent the wheel with more rubber to burn than ever before because they build better business plans and follow more data for better market analysis.

Smart Buying with Foreclosures

When a lender repossesses a home or piece of property it is because the person who borrowed money against the property or piece of real estate has defaulted on the loan. Often a real estate agent finds out about a homeowner in trouble and lets investors know about the potential for it to come up for sale, if the agent can legally disclose the information.

Everything takes place in cycles, and buyers' fears and concerns are no different. Years ago, the foreclosure often scared away potential buyers because the buyer was afraid the property they purchased in foreclosure would be covered in hidden liens or carry some sort of taboo should the buyer who bought in foreclosure later decide to sell the property. Now, foreclosures are a treasure for the talented investor. They represent opportunity and most of the time, they deliver higher profit potential than is typically found in any other real estate investment.

Even though people are amazed to learn that foreclosures are on the rise, investors are not concerned when they contact lenders for recommendations on REO holdings the bank owns. Capable investors begin to prowl the Internet for foreclosures and never stop to wonder why the property ended up with such a stigma attached to it since the housing sector is good and all indications point to its staying that way.

Clever investors know they have to cash in on the foreclosure market if they are going to make the most money in the real estate market. They watch for foreclosures even though they realize they are cashing in on someone else's downfall. They are able to take one man's failure and turn it into their own gain.

Before a home reaches the point of foreclosure, skillful businessmen can approach homeowners and help them avoid an embarrassing foreclosure. Sometimes a real estate agent becomes privy to the information of a homeowner in trouble and will pass along, upon request, the information to investors who may be interested. As an investor, if you discover a homeowner in trouble, there are ways you can help them by helping yourself. Take a look:

- You can help them by buying the house and helping them save an already failing credit score.

- You can come onto the scene by offering a quick sale for

the property owner allowing them to get out from under a debt in a quick and easy manner.

- Buying a distressed property before foreclosure allows the current homeowner to save face and provides the home owner with a more amicable solution than foreclosure.

- In some cases you can help the homeowner save some equity in some cases.

Even with bad or poor credit, the investor can often step in and buy a foreclosure. Keep in mind, with a plan that appears to be better than the plan of foreclosure, many lenders will gladly talk to the investor who wants to step in and take over. A speculator who has the means of financing the foreclosure with excellent credit of their own will, of course, appeal more to the lender prepared to foreclose but regardless of your own credit score, the foreclosure waiting to happen will always listen to you if you have a way to purchase the property.

Buying smart means looking at everything when you buy and in foreclosures, this means checking out everything before closing at the courthouse. One of the reasons the contrarian used to be the only investor who would even consider the foreclosure is because it seemed too risky. The investor who took a chance on the foreclosure wanted a secure investment. He would check everything out at the courthouse before closing to ensure no liens were placed on the property at the last minute. He hired a title company and took out title insurance because he was wise to the fact that the foreclosed property often meant several liens covered the property.

Now, because of courses such as the Carlton Sheets home buying programs and classes to teach investors how to buy smart by looking at all their investing options, the foreclosure is viewed as the investment to make in most circumstances offering the contrarian one more opportunity to buy when the foreclosure presents itself.

Finding the Foreclosure

Sure you can find out about a foreclosure just like everyone else when it hits the local newspaper but why wait until everyone knows about it? There are other ways to find out about a foreclosure, and the best way to discover them is often at the courthouse. You can also check with your local banks and when you do, possibly learn about the REO properties. The REO properties are often those that can re-enter the marketplace and keep the bank or lending institution from losing money when they sell because they are offered through traditional home-selling measures such as through a real estate agent.

Working with Foreclosures

Foreclosures are offered by banks and mortgage companies, HUD housing, the VA, and of course the IRS. Since there are many different sources that fund mortgages, there are many different agencies and individuals who can foreclose on a property.

When an auction due to foreclosure occurs, the property goes on the auction block and it is sold to the person who bids the highest amount for the property. In some instances, a bank or other lender will just take over the property and they will consider this their real estate owned. Many people have heard of the term REO or real estate owned and this is where the term is used. If the bank chooses the REO method instead of foreclosing on the property it can mean more money for the lender later because they can price the real estate to be sold. In a foreclosure auction, whoever bids the highest amount will win the bid and often obtain the property at an incredible savings.

How to Make Foreclosures Work for You

Lenders loan money. Typically they have no interest in maintaining a heavy inventory of REO. They will sell the properties as quickly as they can in most cases, their main objective is to secure a fair price for the REO and ensure that they recoup their perceived loss. Often they know they are not going to recoup the money they lose on a defaulted loan but with a good bid, they are willing to let the real estate go for a fair price. This is where you come in.

Often REO properties are offered for sale to the general public as REO, and the general public must work through a real estate agent to place a bid on the property. The highest bid wins.

Things to Watch for in Foreclosures

Not every foreclosure is a steal. It has always been the general public's belief that foreclosures are great bargains. They are a steal when you can buy them at an auction below appraisal, but doing so is not always possible. The following list will help you when you are looking at buying foreclosures.

- Often there are problems with the property in foreclosure. Do your homework to find out if anyone knows anything about the property.

- Check for easements.

- Check for structural problems in the dwelling.

- Check for land problems.

- See what disclosures are being mentioned about the property.

- Check out all the liens on the property at the courthouse. The auction is meant to satisfy debts but often tax liens travel with the property.

Understand in a foreclosure sale you are going to be expected to pay cash on the day of the sale. This is just another good reason to have a lender in your corner because if you find out about the foreclosure auction only days before the sale, the lender still may be able to provide you with a bank letter that you would use to show you are credit worthy. Still, you need to find out all the particulars of sale by contacting the auctioneer or lender for full details so you are well prepared and know what to do if you want to be considered a serious buyer the day of the auction.

Just a Word about Subject-to Deals

I hear all the hype about subject-to deals and honestly, if you can find one, I say go for it. However, let me explain to you how they are designed to work. If you are buying real estate using a subject-to deal, you are most likely targeting homeowners who are in desperate need to sell. Most of the time, they are one minute away from receiving a foreclosure notice and often they take what they can get. However, this is typically the only time you will be able to sign on a subject-to deal. Why is that?

A person who buys subject-to is buying subject-to the existing financing in place on the house or property. He will want the seller to sign over his deed to him and he will agree to make the payments on the house. He will generally catch up any payments the seller has not made in previous months and walk away with the house. However, the seller will still have the note in his name. The original lenders will not know about the new owner and payments will be sent from the new owner either directly to the lender or through the previous homeowner. Still, the new owner is not on the note.

Now, think about this for a minute. Would you do this? I would not. Would I buy that way? Sure, all day long if someone wants to sell to me and keep their name on the note. Would I sell subject-to? Not on your life.

While subject-to deals enable the investor to come in and pick up a property for a little bit of pocket change, the fact is there will be few takers on this type of deal. Is it a way to creatively finance your purchase? Sure it is but you will not find many of these deals now. Too many of them ended up as deals gone bad.

Many times, people who are looking for the subject-to deals are not in much better shape financially than those getting ready to have foreclosure notices sent to them. With that in mind, why would a seller want to allow a buyer to buy using a subject-to deal when the buyer may not have the money to make the first payment? It is just a bad deal for the seller. However, if any sellers want to sell this way, my number's in the phone book!

Smart Buying When No One Is Buying

Besides foreclosures, there are times when it is smart to buy and then there are times when it would be perceived as just plain dumb. An investor may go into an economically poor area and buy when the town is moving out. He would hope to sell when everyone begins buying again. However, an investor who buys using this mind-set must do so cautiously. There are towns that would not bounce back if their only industry moved away.

There are towns which would be completely desolate if the leading industry in the area just closed its doors. Towns like Kingsport, Tennessee, with Eastman Chemical Company—the largest employer—really do not have much to offer other than Eastman and some smaller, struggling industries in the area. Should the industry move, buying in the town would not be profitable. Michigan's Upper Peninsula never recovered resident interest after the mining and lumber industries pulled out in the 1800s. There are countless towns in Arizona and Texas that are all but deserted. These used to be considered prime buying opportunities but not now.

A contrarian will buy when no one else is buying, but he will not just rush in and buy dumb. In some cases, such as the Kingsport example above, it would be nothing short of foolish to buy in an area when everyone is selling scared because of industry leaving the area. In the case of Michigan's Upper Peninsula area, when the boom was over, it was over and it never came back.

As an investor, you have to weigh many aspects of buying real estate. You have to see what is driving people to sell and see if it is worth your time, effort, and money to buy. If you are familiar with the markets where you are buying real estate, you know what is needed in the area to make the market tick. You know if the housing sector in your area is dependent on the employees who work at one industry or another. You see into the future by recognizing present factors that drive the market in a particular location.

A speculator in a certain area would likely look at some areas as opportunities when a large employer shuts down but it would be much wiser to watch and wait before jumping to buy just because you can buy at 60 percent or 70 percent of the real value of the properties being sold. There are some markets to leave alone until they have dipped as low as they can dip and then they take one more plunge lower before turning.

There is a time to buy distressed and damaged properties, but the time to buy properties in a town where the people cannot leave fast enough probably will not happen. The town is often far from recovery and buying at a discount may cost you more in the long run.

Smart Buying Vacation Rentals

There are many areas where the vacation business is booming. Along the coast, around the world, there are more opportunities than there will ever be investors. In the mountains, there are investment opportunities in the form of ski chalets and romantic cabins. The market is open for the investor in vacations and the savvy investor sees promise here.

Oceanfront properties around the world are among the highest valued properties on the market today and for years, history will show these properties have been overpriced while still climbing in most areas. The contrarian buys in areas when the market seems to have run its course and hopes vacationers will continue to come, and the investor-contrarian continues to buy when the market drops.

A contrarian investor will go into a beach area and buy properties others would never consider. He might buy a block or two off the beach when the fixer-upper or handyman special becomes available. He will remodel the home, perhaps adding a roof-top sundeck if ocean views are available, fencing in the area for a pet-friendly rental near the ocean, or putting in a swimming pool. Before you know it, his property is commanding almost as much as the oceanfront owners' and he has a better investment because his insurance is lower and his property sets off the beach enough that the risk of a natural disaster is less compared to his beachfront neighbors.

Best of all, the investor who buys beach property near but not on the beach will face lower sales prices than the sister properties set directly oceanfront. For $350,000 an oceanfront condo may have direct oceanfront views but the condo two streets back offers views of the ocean and is directly overlooking the pool with twice the square footage. The price tag is also considered cheap for the area—an astonishingly low $99,000.

Investors who begin to test the waters by purchasing investment properties in areas where vacationers frequently visit find that in most circumstances, owning a rental in the general vicinity proves far more profitable in the long run. For instance, in Colorado, chalets situated directly on the mountain offering skiers the ability to ski right onto the slopes tend to be expensive when they come up for sale. However, in most of the highly populated ski towns, the investor knows tourists will be willing to drive to the slopes and will look for savings away from the slope-fronts.

Vacation rentals are great investment opportunities. The investor who knows "close-in" or "close in proximity to" can find great deals in their vacation rentals and they look for them. Contrarian investors know they can save money by buying property off the beach or away from the main attraction in any given area. They pay a fraction of the price and realize more square footage. The properties will often be in better shape and will not lose that many renters due to location because they will add to the overall appeal of the property to make up for what they lack in location.

Smart investors find areas booming with vacationers and then try to purchase during the off-season, if there is one. The smart entrepreneur will rush into town and find the property owner or owners who are pricing their properties for a "quick sale" or they will try to find the distressed property. The investor who knows the vacation area where he will be buying, recognizes the best time to buy in the area, and when he has the prime opportunity he will make an offer on a profitable vacation rental.

Chapter Ten

The Financing You Need

T he longer you are in real estate as an investor, the more opportunities you will find to finance your real estate deals creatively. You will find ways to finance your transactions and ways to use your options to put together the most lucrative package for your loan needs.

FHA and VA Loans

Federal Housing Authority (FHA) and Veterans Administration (VA) loans have often been considered the easiest way to afford and finance your dreams, but often there are stipulations about whether you can finance an investment property and use a VA or FHA loan, but FHA and VA loans can be the best way to finance your primary residence.

FHA stands for Federal Housing Association and has been around since 1934 when the government recognized an affordable housing need. The FHA helped minimize the national housing problem at the time. The FHA loan has provided an alternative to conventional loans by providing fewer loan requirements and by appealing to minorities, first-time home buyers, and buyers with credit problems.

What you need to know about the FHA Loan:

- Easier to secure than conventional loans

- Can be secured not only by first-time home buyers but by anyone meeting the loan requirements set by the FHA

- FHA loans require less money down than most loans

- Handy-man specials normally do not qualify under the strict guidelines for the FHA because the housing program was designed more for the home owner who would live in the home as a primary residence and not for the investor

- Owner must occupy the home secured by the FHA loan

- Loan amounts for FHA loans can vary

- The FHA loans are assumable, but they still go through a process, and each borrower will have to qualify on their own merit in most cases

- Foreclosures and other properties in financial distress often qualify for FHA loans

- Houses must appraise for the purchase price in a FHA loan

Because of stipulations, FHA loans are not viewed as the best means to use for creative financing, yet they can be used creatively. Borrowers can borrow the money for the down payment for a FHA loan and sellers often loan the money for the down payment, but the down payment loan is reflected in a different manner in most cases.

Another government-secured loan is the Veterans Administration Loan. The VA loan is in place for veterans to use. There are some stipulations involving active duty as well as other qualifications in place for a veteran to secure the loan. Still, the VA loan offers veterans an appealing loan option. Following are things to expect with the VA loan:

- You have to qualify for the loan based on veteran or active duty status

- There are qualifying periods which change from time to time

- The approval time for the VA loan is shorter than in years past

- The VA loan offers low interest rates, no down payment options, and no pre-payment penalties as well as an assumable option

A VA or FHA loan can be the answer to a young buyer's investment goals and can be used for the primary residence of a seasoned real estate investor. Still, it is important to remember that in most cases the buyer must occupy the residence and even if the loan is assumable, the lender is still in full control over who assumes the note down the road. The assumable loan feature just makes it easier to sell the property down the road because it can save potential buyers time and money on a transfer of sale.

Assumable Mortgages

Assumable mortgages are great tools to use when creatively financing your real estate investments. For starters, they are easier to transfer from the seller to the buyer if the buyer is credit worthy and meets the lender's requirements. Some assumable mortgages even transfer from the seller to the buyer with the original loan terms that can save the buyer time and money. Still, a buyer's credit will have some weight in whether the assumable mortgage is easily transferred. Credit checks will be conducted and proof of income showing the buyer can afford the property will be required. Terms of the assumable mortgage can vary from the original terms and often the terms will be less attractive than the original loan terms in which case it would be more advantageous for the buyer to obtain his or her own note for the property.

As a seller, you want to ensure you are not liable in any way for the property or the note after you allow the buyer to assume the property. To cut all ties, you should request a release form. The lender should be able to provide you with one before closing so you can take a look at it with your attorney.

FHA and VA assumable loans can be attractive to buyers but assumable VA mortgage loans are only assumable by a veteran, and there are several other stipulations and guidelines to the VA assumable loans just like any other assumable loan. Take the time to know what a future buyer may need to know about your assumable mortgage. It will help you in the future to ask questions when it comes time for you to sell to the next home owner of your house.

Wraparound Financing

Creatively finance enough properties and you will learn how to use the wraparound mortgage. The wraparound mortgage is the same as the all-inclusive mortgage. Investors in real estate will use the wraparound. Below is a good example of a wraparound mortgage.

Wraparound Mortgage Example

Sharon has no cash on hand to close on her dream home, but she has a seller who is willing to help. The home is on the market for $110,000 and the current seller has a mortgage for $75,000 on the property. Sharon's parents give her $10,000 and suddenly the seller will look at the wraparound mortgage to help Sharon buy the home. Sharon qualifies for a conventional loan but it requires a down payment of about $22,000.

Here is how Sharon saves the deal: the seller owes $75,000 and Sharon has $10,000 but that leaves a difference of $25,000 so the seller offers to finance the entire $100,000. Since Sharon suggests a wraparound mortgage to avoid the need for a $22,000 down payment, she understands the risks and has her attorney draw up the paperwork for a wraparound mortgage. The seller will continue making monthly payments and will charge Sharon a bit more per month to ensure he is making a little bit extra money for his troubles, and Sharon and the seller wrap together the two mortgages: the old mortgage and Sharon's new one.

Finding the Best Way to Finance the Property You Want to Buy

Unless your last name is Rockefeller, you have some financial ups and downs, especially when you are under 35. When things are a bit too volatile for comfort, you need to find some of the best ways to finance your investments so you are still accumulating properties when the market is a buyers' market and trends indicate it is time to buy.

Below, take a look at three different scenarios. For illustrative purposes, the loan amount is $150,000 and the interest rate is 8 percent. The first is a conventional loan financed and amortized over 30 years using a bank. The second is a conventional loan financed and amortized over 15 years using a bank, and the third is a purchase-money mortgage financed over five years with a lower interest rate and a balloon payment. These examples show why it is often crucial in finding a seller to carry the paper on your investments.

In Example One below, at the end of the note, the total repaid will be $396,234 based on a 30-year note amortized over 30 years at 8 percent which means the buyer/investor will pay a total of $246,234.00 in interest.

Pmt	Principal	Interest	Cm Prin	Cm Int	Prin Bal
1	100.65	1000.00	100.65	1000.00	149899.35
2	101.32	999.33	201.97	1999.33	149798.03
3	102.00	998.65	303.97	2997.98	149696.03
4	102.68	997.97	406.65	3995.95	149593.35
5	103.36	997.29	510.01	4993.24	149489.99
6	104.05	996.60	614.06	5989.84	149385.94
7	104.74	995.91	718.80	6985.75	149281.20

8	105.44	995.21	824.24	7980.96	149175.76
9	106.14	994.51	930.38	8975.47	149069.62
10	106.85	993.80	1037.23	9969.27	148962.77
11	107.56	993.09	1144.79	10962.36	148855.21
12	108.28	992.37	1253.07	11954.73	148746.93

13	109.00	991.65	1362.07	12946.38	148637.93
14	109.73	990.92	1471.80	13937.30	148528.20
15	110.46	990.19	1582.26	14927.49	148417.74
16	111.20	989.45	1693.46	15916.94	148306.54
17	111.94	988.71	1805.40	16905.65	148194.60
18	112.69	987.96	1918.09	17893.61	148081.91
19	113.44	987.21	2031.53	18880.82	147968.47
20	114.19	986.46	2145.72	19867.28	147854.28
21	114.95	985.70	2260.67	20852.98	147739.33
22	115.72	984.93	2376.39	21837.91	147623.61
23	116.49	984.16	2492.88	22822.07	147507.12
24	117.27	983.38	2610.15	23805.45	147389.85

25	118.05	982.60	2728.20	24788.05	147271.80
26	118.84	981.81	2847.04	25769.86	147152.96
27	119.63	981.02	2966.67	26750.88	147033.33
28	120.43	980.22	3087.10	27731.10	146912.90
29	121.23	979.42	3208.33	28710.52	146791.67
30	122.04	978.61	3330.37	29689.13	146669.63
31	122.85	977.80	3453.22	30666.93	146546.78
32	123.67	976.98	3576.89	31643.91	146423.11
33	124.50	976.15	3701.39	32620.06	146298.61
34	125.33	975.32	3826.72	33595.38	146173.28
35	126.16	974.49	3952.88	34569.87	146047.12
36	127.00	973.65	4079.88	35543.52	145920.12

37	127.85	972.80	4207.73	36516.32	145792.27

38	128.70	971.95	4336.43	37488.27	145663.57
39	129.56	971.09	4465.99	38459.36	145534.01
40	130.42	970.23	4596.41	39429.59	145403.59
41	131.29	969.36	4727.70	40398.95	145272.30
42	132.17	968.48	4859.87	41367.43	145140.13
43	133.05	967.60	4992.92	42335.03	145007.08
44	133.94	966.71	5126.86	43301.74	144873.14
45	134.83	965.82	5261.69	44267.56	144738.31
46	135.73	964.92	5397.42	45232.48	144602.58
47	136.63	964.02	5534.05	46196.50	144465.95
48	137.54	963.11	5671.59	47159.61	144328.41

49	138.46	962.19	5810.05	48121.80	144189.95
50	139.38	961.27	5949.43	49083.07	144050.57
51	140.31	960.34	6089.74	50043.41	143910.26
52	141.25	959.40	6230.99	51002.81	143769.01
53	142.19	958.46	6373.18	51961.27	143626.82
54	143.14	957.51	6516.32	52918.78	143483.68
55	144.09	956.56	6660.41	53875.34	143339.59
56	145.05	955.60	6805.46	54830.94	143194.54
57	146.02	954.63	6951.48	55785.57	143048.52
58	146.99	953.66	7098.47	56739.23	142901.53
59	147.97	952.68	7246.44	57691.91	142753.56
60	148.96	951.69	7395.40	58643.60	142604.60

61	149.95	950.70	7545.35	59594.30	142454.65
62	150.95	949.70	7696.30	60544.00	142303.70
63	151.96	948.69	7848.26	61492.69	142151.74
64	152.97	947.68	8001.23	62440.37	141998.77
65	153.99	946.66	8155.22	63387.03	141844.78
66	155.02	945.63	8310.24	64332.66	141689.76
67	156.05	944.60	8466.29	65277.26	141533.71
68	157.09	943.56	8623.38	66220.82	141376.62

69	158.14	942.51	8781.52	67163.33	141218.48
70	159.19	941.46	8940.71	68104.79	141059.29
71	160.25	940.40	9100.96	69045.19	140899.04
72	161.32	939.33	9262.28	69984.52	140737.72

73	162.40	938.25	9424.68	70922.77	140575.32
74	163.48	937.17	9588.16	71859.94	140411.84
75	164.57	936.08	9752.73	72796.02	140247.27
76	165.67	934.98	9918.40	73731.00	140081.60
77	166.77	933.88	10085.17	74664.88	139914.83
78	167.88	932.77	10253.05	75597.65	139746.95
79	169.00	931.65	10422.05	76529.30	139577.95
80	170.13	930.52	10592.18	77459.82	139407.82
81	171.26	929.39	10763.44	78389.21	139236.56
82	172.41	928.24	10935.85	79317.45	139064.15
83	173.56	927.09	11109.41	80244.54	138890.59
84	174.71	925.94	11284.12	81170.48	138715.88

85	175.88	924.77	11460.00	82095.25	138540.00
86	177.05	923.60	11637.05	83018.85	138362.95
87	178.23	922.42	11815.28	83941.27	138184.72
88	179.42	921.23	11994.70	84862.50	138005.30
89	180.61	920.04	12175.31	85782.54	137824.69
90	181.82	918.83	12357.13	86701.37	137642.87
91	183.03	917.62	12540.16	87618.99	137459.84
92	184.25	916.40	12724.41	88535.39	137275.59
93	185.48	915.17	12909.89	89450.56	137090.11
94	186.72	913.93	13096.61	90364.49	136903.39
95	187.96	912.69	13284.57	91277.18	136715.43
96	189.21	911.44	13473.78	92188.62	136526.22

97	190.48	910.17	13664.26	93098.79	136335.74
98	191.75	908.90	13856.01	94007.69	136143.99

99	193.02	907.63	14049.03	94915.32	135950.97
100	194.31	906.34	14243.34	95821.66	135756.66
101	195.61	905.04	14438.95	96726.70	135561.05
102	196.91	903.74	14635.86	97630.44	135364.14
103	198.22	902.43	14834.08	98532.87	135165.92
104	199.54	901.11	15033.62	99433.98	134966.38
105	200.87	899.78	15234.49	100333.76	134765.51
106	202.21	898.44	15436.70	101232.20	134563.30
107	203.56	897.09	15640.26	102129.29	134359.74
108	204.92	895.73	15845.18	103025.02	134154.82

109	206.28	894.37	16051.46	103919.39	133948.54
110	207.66	892.99	16259.12	104812.38	133740.88
111	209.04	891.61	16468.16	105703.99	133531.84
112	210.44	890.21	16678.60	106594.20	133321.40
113	211.84	888.81	16890.44	107483.01	133109.56
114	213.25	887.40	17103.69	108370.41	132896.31
115	214.67	885.98	17318.36	109256.39	132681.64
116	216.11	884.54	17534.47	110140.93	132465.53
117	217.55	883.10	17752.02	111024.03	132247.98
118	219.00	881.65	17971.02	111905.68	132028.98
119	220.46	880.19	18191.48	112785.87	131808.52
120	221.93	878.72	18413.41	113664.59	131586.59

121	223.41	877.24	18636.82	114541.83	131363.18
122	224.90	875.75	18861.72	115417.58	131138.28
123	226.39	874.26	19088.11	116291.84	130911.89
124	227.90	872.75	19316.01	117164.59	130683.99
125	229.42	871.23	19545.43	118035.82	130454.57
126	230.95	869.70	19776.38	118905.52	130223.62
127	232.49	868.16	20008.87	119773.68	129991.13
128	234.04	866.61	20242.91	120640.29	129757.09
129	235.60	865.05	20478.51	121505.34	129521.49

130	237.17	863.48	20715.68	122368.82	129284.32
131	238.75	861.90	20954.43	123230.72	129045.57
132	240.35	860.30	21194.78	124091.02	128805.22

133	241.95	858.70	21436.73	124949.72	128563.27
134	243.56	857.09	21680.29	125806.81	128319.71
135	245.19	855.46	21925.48	126662.27	128074.52
136	246.82	853.83	22172.30	127516.10	127827.70
137	248.47	852.18	22420.77	128368.28	127579.23
138	250.12	850.53	22670.89	129218.81	127329.11
139	251.79	848.86	22922.68	130067.67	127077.32
140	253.47	847.18	23176.15	130914.85	126823.85
141	255.16	845.49	23431.31	131760.34	126568.69
142	256.86	843.79	23688.17	132604.13	126311.83
143	258.57	842.08	23946.74	133446.21	126053.26
144	260.29	840.36	24207.03	134286.57	125792.97

145	262.03	838.62	24469.06	135125.19	125530.94
146	263.78	836.87	24732.84	135962.06	125267.16
147	265.54	835.11	24998.38	136797.17	125001.62
148	267.31	833.34	25265.69	137630.51	124734.31
149	269.09	831.56	25534.78	138462.07	124465.22
150	270.88	829.77	25805.66	139291.84	124194.34
151	272.69	827.96	26078.35	140119.80	123921.65
152	274.51	826.14	26352.86	140945.94	123647.14
153	276.34	824.31	26629.20	141770.25	123370.80
154	278.18	822.47	26907.38	142592.72	123092.62
155	280.03	820.62	27187.41	143413.34	122812.59
156	281.90	818.75	27469.31	144232.09	122530.69

157	283.78	816.87	27753.09	145048.96	122246.91
158	285.67	814.98	28038.76	145863.94	121961.24
159	287.58	813.07	28326.34	146677.01	121673.66

160	289.49	811.16	28615.83	147488.17	121384.17
161	291.42	809.23	28907.25	148297.40	121092.75
162	293.36	807.29	29200.61	149104.69	120799.39
163	295.32	805.33	29495.93	149910.02	120504.07
164	297.29	803.36	29793.22	150713.38	120206.78
165	299.27	801.38	30092.49	151514.76	119907.51
166	301.27	799.38	30393.76	152314.14	119606.24
167	303.28	797.37	30697.04	153111.51	119302.96
168	305.30	795.35	31002.34	153906.86	118997.66

169	307.33	793.32	31309.67	154700.18	118690.33
170	309.38	791.27	31619.05	155491.45	118380.95
171	311.44	789.21	31930.49	156280.66	118069.51
172	313.52	787.13	32244.01	157067.79	117755.99
173	315.61	785.04	32559.62	157852.83	117440.38
174	317.71	782.94	32877.33	158635.77	117122.67
175	319.83	780.82	33197.16	159416.59	116802.84
176	321.96	778.69	33519.12	160195.28	116480.88
177	324.11	776.54	33843.23	160971.82	116156.77
178	326.27	774.38	34169.50	161746.20	115830.50
179	328.45	772.20	34497.95	162518.40	115502.05
180	330.64	770.01	34828.59	163288.41	115171.41

181	332.84	767.81	35161.43	164056.22	114838.57
182	335.06	765.59	35496.49	164821.81	114503.51
183	337.29	763.36	35833.78	165585.17	114166.22
184	339.54	761.11	36173.32	166346.28	113826.68
185	341.81	758.84	36515.13	167105.12	113484.87
186	344.08	756.57	36859.21	167861.69	113140.79
187	346.38	754.27	37205.59	168615.96	112794.41
188	348.69	751.96	37554.28	169367.92	112445.72
189	351.01	749.64	37905.29	170117.56	112094.71

190	353.35	747.30	38258.64	170864.86	111741.36
191	355.71	744.94	38614.35	171609.80	111385.65
192	358.08	742.57	38972.43	172352.37	111027.57

193	360.47	740.18	39332.90	173092.55	110667.10
194	362.87	737.78	39695.77	173830.33	110304.23
195	365.29	735.36	40061.06	174565.69	109938.94
196	367.72	732.93	40428.78	175298.62	109571.22
197	370.18	730.47	40798.96	176029.09	109201.04
198	372.64	728.01	41171.60	176757.10	108828.40
199	375.13	725.52	41546.73	177482.62	108453.27
200	377.63	723.02	41924.36	178205.64	108075.64
201	380.15	720.50	42304.51	178926.14	107695.49
202	382.68	717.97	42687.19	179644.11	107312.81
203	385.23	715.42	43072.42	180359.53	106927.58
204	387.80	712.85	43460.22	181072.38	106539.78

205	390.38	710.27	43850.60	181782.65	106149.40
206	392.99	707.66	44243.59	182490.31	105756.41
207	395.61	705.04	44639.20	183195.35	105360.80
208	398.24	702.41	45037.44	183897.76	104962.56
209	400.90	699.75	45438.34	184597.51	104561.66
210	403.57	697.08	45841.91	185294.59	104158.09
211	406.26	694.39	46248.17	185988.98	103751.83
212	408.97	691.68	46657.14	186680.66	103342.86
213	411.70	688.95	47068.84	187369.61	102931.16
214	414.44	686.21	47483.28	188055.82	102516.72
215	417.21	683.44	47900.49	188739.26	102099.51
216	419.99	680.66	48320.48	189419.92	101679.52

217	422.79	677.86	48743.27	190097.78	101256.73
218	425.61	675.04	49168.88	190772.82	100831.12

219	428.44	672.21	49597.32	191445.03	100402.68
220	431.30	669.35	50028.62	192114.38	99971.38
221	434.17	666.48	50462.79	192780.86	99537.21
222	437.07	663.58	50899.86	193444.44	99100.14
223	439.98	660.67	51339.84	194105.11	98660.16
224	442.92	657.73	51782.76	194762.84	98217.24
225	445.87	654.78	52228.63	195417.62	97771.37
226	448.84	651.81	52677.47	196069.43	97322.53
227	451.83	648.82	53129.30	196718.25	96870.70
228	454.85	645.80	53584.15	197364.05	96415.85

229	457.88	642.77	54042.03	198006.82	95957.97
230	460.93	639.72	54502.96	198646.54	95497.04
231	464.00	636.65	54966.96	199283.19	95033.04
232	467.10	633.55	55434.06	199916.74	94565.94
233	470.21	630.44	55904.27	200547.18	94095.73
234	473.35	627.30	56377.62	201174.48	93622.38
235	476.50	624.15	56854.12	201798.63	93145.88
236	479.68	620.97	57333.80	202419.60	92666.20
237	482.88	617.77	57816.68	203037.37	92183.32
238	486.09	614.56	58302.77	203651.93	91697.23
239	489.34	611.31	58792.11	204263.24	91207.89
240	492.60	608.05	59284.71	204871.29	90715.29

241	495.88	604.77	59780.59	205476.06	90219.41
242	499.19	601.46	60279.78	206077.52	89720.22
243	502.52	598.13	60782.30	206675.65	89217.70
244	505.87	594.78	61288.17	207270.43	88711.83
245	509.24	591.41	61797.41	207861.84	88202.59
246	512.63	588.02	62310.04	208449.86	87689.96
247	516.05	584.60	62826.09	209034.46	87173.91
248	519.49	581.16	63345.58	209615.62	86654.42

249	522.95	577.70	63868.53	210193.32	86131.47
250	526.44	574.21	64394.97	210767.53	85605.03
251	529.95	570.70	64924.92	211338.23	85075.08
252	533.48	567.17	65458.40	211905.40	84541.60

253	537.04	563.61	65995.44	212469.01	84004.56
254	540.62	560.03	66536.06	213029.04	83463.94
255	544.22	556.43	67080.28	213585.47	82919.72
256	547.85	552.80	67628.13	214138.27	82371.87
257	551.50	549.15	68179.63	214687.42	81820.37
258	555.18	545.47	68734.81	215232.89	81265.19
259	558.88	541.77	69293.69	215774.66	80706.31
260	562.61	538.04	69856.30	216312.70	80143.70
261	566.36	534.29	70422.66	216846.99	79577.34
262	570.13	530.52	70992.79	217377.51	79007.21
263	573.94	526.71	71566.73	217904.22	78433.27
264	577.76	522.89	72144.49	218427.11	77855.51

265	581.61	519.04	72726.10	218946.15	77273.90
266	585.49	515.16	73311.59	219461.31	76688.41
267	589.39	511.26	73900.98	219972.57	76099.02
268	593.32	507.33	74494.30	220479.90	75505.70
269	597.28	503.37	75091.58	220983.27	74908.42
270	601.26	499.39	75692.84	221482.66	74307.16
271	605.27	495.38	76298.11	221978.04	73701.89
272	609.30	491.35	76907.41	222469.39	73092.59
273	613.37	487.28	77520.78	222956.67	72479.22
274	617.46	483.19	78138.24	223439.86	71861.76
275	621.57	479.08	78759.81	223918.94	71240.19
276	625.72	474.93	79385.53	224393.87	70614.47

277	629.89	470.76	80015.42	224864.63	69984.58

278	634.09	466.56	80649.51	225331.19	69350.49
279	638.31	462.34	81287.82	225793.53	68712.18
280	642.57	458.08	81930.39	226251.61	68069.61
281	646.85	453.80	82577.24	226705.41	67422.76
282	651.16	449.49	83228.40	227154.90	66771.60
283	655.51	445.14	83883.91	227600.04	66116.09
284	659.88	440.77	84543.79	228040.81	65456.21
285	664.28	436.37	85208.07	228477.18	64791.93
286	668.70	431.95	85876.77	228909.13	64123.23
287	673.16	427.49	86549.93	229336.62	63450.07
288	677.65	423.00	87227.58	229759.62	62772.42

289	682.17	418.48	87909.75	230178.10	62090.25
290	686.72	413.93	88596.47	230592.03	61403.53
291	691.29	409.36	89287.76	231001.39	60712.24
292	695.90	404.75	89983.66	231406.14	60016.34
293	700.54	400.11	90684.20	231806.25	59315.80
294	705.21	395.44	91389.41	232201.69	58610.59
295	709.91	390.74	92099.32	232592.43	57900.68
296	714.65	386.00	92813.97	232978.43	57186.03
297	719.41	381.24	93533.38	233359.67	56466.62
298	724.21	376.44	94257.59	233736.11	55742.41
299	729.03	371.62	94986.62	234107.73	55013.38
300	733.89	366.76	95720.51	234474.49	54279.49

301	738.79	361.86	96459.30	234836.35	53540.70
302	743.71	356.94	97203.01	235193.29	52796.99
303	748.67	351.98	97951.68	235545.27	52048.32
304	753.66	346.99	98705.34	235892.26	51294.66
305	758.69	341.96	99464.03	236234.22	50535.97
306	763.74	336.91	100227.77	236571.13	49772.23
307	768.84	331.81	100996.61	236902.94	49003.39
308	773.96	326.69	101770.57	237229.63	48229.43

309	779.12	321.53	102549.69	237551.16	47450.31
310	784.31	316.34	103334.00	237867.50	46666.00
311	789.54	311.11	104123.54	238178.61	45876.46
312	794.81	305.84	104918.35	238484.45	45081.65

313	800.11	300.54	105718.46	238784.99	44281.54
314	805.44	295.21	106523.90	239080.20	43476.10
315	810.81	289.84	107334.71	239370.04	42665.29
316	816.21	284.44	108150.92	239654.48	41849.08
317	821.66	278.99	108972.58	239933.47	41027.42
318	827.13	273.52	109799.71	240206.99	40200.29
319	832.65	268.00	110632.36	240474.99	39367.64
320	838.20	262.45	111470.56	240737.44	38529.44
321	843.79	256.86	112314.35	240994.30	37685.65
322	849.41	251.24	113163.76	241245.54	36836.24
323	855.08	245.57	114018.84	241491.11	35981.16
324	860.78	239.87	114879.62	241730.98	35120.38

325	866.51	234.14	115746.13	241965.12	34253.87
326	872.29	228.36	116618.42	242193.48	33381.58
327	878.11	222.54	117496.53	242416.02	32503.47
328	883.96	216.69	118380.49	242632.71	31619.51
329	889.85	210.80	119270.34	242843.51	30729.66
330	895.79	204.86	120166.13	243048.37	29833.87
331	901.76	198.89	121067.89	243247.26	28932.11
332	907.77	192.88	121975.66	243440.14	28024.34
333	913.82	186.83	122889.48	243626.97	27110.52
334	919.91	180.74	123809.39	243807.71	26190.61
335	926.05	174.60	124735.44	243982.31	25264.56
336	932.22	168.43	125667.66	244150.74	24332.34

337	938.43	162.22	126606.09	244312.96	23393.91
338	944.69	155.96	127550.78	244468.92	22449.22

339	950.99	149.66	128501.77	244618.58	21498.23
340	957.33	143.32	129459.10	244761.90	20540.90
341	963.71	136.94	130422.81	244898.84	19577.19
342	970.14	130.51	131392.95	245029.35	18607.05
343	976.60	124.05	132369.55	245153.40	17630.45
344	983.11	117.54	133352.66	245270.94	16647.34
345	989.67	110.98	134342.33	245381.92	15657.67
346	996.27	104.38	135338.60	245486.30	14661.40
347	1002.91	97.74	136341.51	245584.04	13658.49
348	1009.59	91.06	137351.10	245675.10	12648.90

349	1016.32	84.33	138367.42	245759.43	11632.58
350	1023.10	77.55	139390.52	245836.98	10609.48
351	1029.92	70.73	140420.44	245907.71	9579.56
352	1036.79	63.86	141457.23	245971.57	8542.77
353	1043.70	56.95	142500.93	246028.52	7499.07
354	1050.66	49.99	143551.59	246078.51	6448.41
355	1057.66	42.99	144609.25	246121.50	5390.75
356	1064.71	35.94	145673.96	246157.44	4326.04
357	1071.81	28.84	146745.77	246186.28	3254.23
358	1078.96	21.69	147824.73	246207.97	2175.27
359	1086.15	14.50	148910.88	246222.47	1089.12
360	*1089.12	7.26	150000.00	246229.73	0.00

In Example Two below, at the end of the note, the total repaid will be $258,026.40 based on a 15-year note amortized over 15 years at 8 percent which means the buyer/investor will pay a total of $108,026.40 in interest. Keep in mind, as an investor looking to make a sound investment, there is a big difference in paying $246,234 in interest and $108,026.40. In fact, by financing the home over 15 years rather than 30 years, you will save $138,207.60 and the payment difference? On 15 years, you pay $1,433.48 and on 30 years, you pay $1,100.65 for a difference of $332.83 per month. Still, it is worth it to most people to pay the extra payment per month to avoid paying an additional $138,207.60 for the property.

Pmt	Principal	Interest	Cm Prin	Cm Int	Prin Bal
1	433.48	1000.00	433.48	1000.00	149566.52
2	436.37	997.11	869.85	1997.11	149130.15
3	439.28	994.20	1309.13	2991.31	148690.87
4	442.21	991.27	1751.34	3982.58	148248.66
5	445.16	988.32	2196.50	4970.90	147803.50
6	448.12	985.36	2644.62	5956.26	147355.38
7	451.11	982.37	3095.73	6938.63	146904.27
8	454.12	979.36	3549.85	7917.99	146450.15
9	457.15	976.33	4007.00	8894.32	145993.00
10	460.19	973.29	4467.19	9867.61	145532.81
11	463.26	970.22	4930.45	10837.83	145069.55
12	466.35	967.13	5396.80	11804.96	144603.20
13	469.46	964.02	5866.26	12768.98	144133.74
14	472.59	960.89	6338.85	13729.87	143661.15
15	475.74	957.74	6814.59	14687.61	143185.41
16	478.91	954.57	7293.50	15642.18	142706.50
17	482.10	951.38	7775.60	16593.56	142224.40
18	485.32	948.16	8260.92	17541.72	141739.08
19	488.55	944.93	8749.47	18486.65	141250.53
20	491.81	941.67	9241.28	19428.32	140758.72
21	495.09	938.39	9736.37	20366.71	140263.63
22	498.39	935.09	10234.76	21301.80	139765.24
23	501.71	931.77	10736.47	22233.57	139263.53
24	505.06	928.42	11241.53	23161.99	138758.47
25	508.42	925.06	11749.95	24087.05	138250.05
26	511.81	921.67	12261.76	25008.72	137738.24

27	515.23	918.25	12776.99	25926.97	137223.01
28	518.66	914.82	13295.65	26841.79	136704.35
29	522.12	911.36	13817.77	27753.15	136182.23
30	525.60	907.88	14343.37	28661.03	135656.63
31	529.10	904.38	14872.47	29565.41	135127.53
32	532.63	900.85	15405.10	30466.26	134594.90
33	536.18	897.30	15941.28	31363.56	134058.72
34	539.76	893.72	16481.04	32257.28	133518.96
35	543.35	890.13	17024.39	33147.41	132975.61
36	546.98	886.50	17571.37	34033.91	132428.63

37	550.62	882.86	18121.99	34916.77	131878.01
38	554.29	879.19	18676.28	35795.96	131323.72
39	557.99	875.49	19234.27	36671.45	130765.73
40	561.71	871.77	19795.98	37543.22	130204.02
41	565.45	868.03	20361.43	38411.25	129638.57
42	569.22	864.26	20930.65	39275.51	129069.35
43	573.02	860.46	21503.67	40135.97	128496.33
44	576.84	856.64	22080.51	40992.61	127919.49
45	580.68	852.80	22661.19	41845.41	127338.81
46	584.55	848.93	23245.74	42694.34	126754.26
47	588.45	845.03	23834.19	43539.37	126165.81
48	592.37	841.11	24426.56	44380.48	125573.44

49	596.32	837.16	25022.88	45217.64	124977.12
50	600.30	833.18	25623.18	46050.82	124376.82
51	604.30	829.18	26227.48	46880.00	123772.52
52	608.33	825.15	26835.81	47705.15	123164.19
53	612.39	821.09	27448.20	48526.24	122551.80
54	616.47	817.01	28064.67	49343.25	121935.33
55	620.58	812.90	28685.25	50156.15	121314.75
56	624.72	808.76	29309.97	50964.91	120690.03
57	628.88	804.60	29938.85	51769.51	120061.15

58	633.07	800.41	30571.92	52569.92	119428.08
59	637.29	796.19	31209.21	53366.11	118790.79
60	641.54	791.94	31850.75	54158.05	118149.25

61	645.82	787.66	32496.57	54945.71	117503.43
62	650.12	783.36	33146.69	55729.07	116853.31
63	654.46	779.02	33801.15	56508.09	116198.85
64	658.82	774.66	34459.97	57282.75	115540.03
65	663.21	770.27	35123.18	58053.02	114876.82
66	667.63	765.85	35790.81	58818.87	114209.19
67	672.09	761.39	36462.90	59580.26	113537.10
68	676.57	756.91	37139.47	60337.17	112860.53
69	681.08	752.40	37820.55	61089.57	112179.45
70	685.62	747.86	38506.17	61837.43	111493.83
71	690.19	743.29	39196.36	62580.72	110803.64
72	694.79	738.69	39891.15	63319.41	110108.85

73	699.42	734.06	40590.57	64053.47	109409.43
74	704.08	729.40	41294.65	64782.87	108705.35
75	708.78	724.70	42003.43	65507.57	107996.57
76	713.50	719.98	42716.93	66227.55	107283.07
77	718.26	715.22	43435.19	66942.77	106564.81
78	723.05	710.43	44158.24	67653.20	105841.76
79	727.87	705.61	44886.11	68358.81	105113.89
80	732.72	700.76	45618.83	69059.57	104381.17
81	737.61	695.87	46356.44	69755.44	103643.56
82	742.52	690.96	47098.96	70446.40	102901.04
83	747.47	686.01	47846.43	71132.41	102153.57
84	752.46	681.02	48598.89	71813.43	101401.11

85	757.47	676.01	49356.36	72489.44	100643.64
86	762.52	670.96	50118.88	73160.40	99881.12
87	767.61	665.87	50886.49	73826.27	99113.51

88	772.72	660.76	51659.21	74487.03	98340.79
89	777.87	655.61	52437.08	75142.64	97562.92
90	783.06	650.42	53220.14	75793.06	96779.86
91	788.28	645.20	54008.42	76438.26	95991.58
92	793.54	639.94	54801.96	77078.20	95198.04
93	798.83	634.65	55600.79	77712.85	94399.21
94	804.15	629.33	56404.94	78342.18	93595.06
95	809.51	623.97	57214.45	78966.15	92785.55
96	814.91	618.57	58029.36	79584.72	91970.64

97	820.34	613.14	58849.70	80197.86	91150.30
98	825.81	607.67	59675.51	80805.53	90324.49
99	831.32	602.16	60506.83	81407.69	89493.17
100	836.86	596.62	61343.69	82004.31	88656.31
101	842.44	591.04	62186.13	82595.35	87813.87
102	848.05	585.43	63034.18	83180.78	86965.82
103	853.71	579.77	63887.89	83760.55	86112.11
104	859.40	574.08	64747.29	84334.63	85252.71
105	865.13	568.35	65612.42	84902.98	84387.58
106	870.90	562.58	66483.32	85465.56	83516.68
107	876.70	556.78	67360.02	86022.34	82639.98
108	882.55	550.93	68242.57	86573.27	81757.43

109	888.43	545.05	69131.00	87118.32	80869.00
110	894.35	539.13	70025.35	87657.45	79974.65
111	900.32	533.16	70925.67	88190.61	79074.33
112	906.32	527.16	71831.99	88717.77	78168.01
113	912.36	521.12	72744.35	89238.89	77255.65
114	918.44	515.04	73662.79	89753.93	76337.21
115	924.57	508.91	74587.36	90262.84	75412.64
116	930.73	502.75	75518.09	90765.59	74481.91
117	936.93	496.55	76455.02	91262.14	73544.98

118	943.18	490.30	77398.20	91752.44	72601.80
119	949.47	484.01	78347.67	92236.45	71652.33
120	955.80	477.68	79303.47	92714.13	70696.53

121	962.17	471.31	80265.64	93185.44	69734.36
122	968.58	464.90	81234.22	93650.34	68765.78
123	975.04	458.44	82209.26	94108.78	67790.74
124	981.54	451.94	83190.80	94560.72	66809.20
125	988.09	445.39	84178.89	95006.11	65821.11
126	994.67	438.81	85173.56	95444.92	64826.44
127	1001.30	432.18	86174.86	95877.10	63825.14
128	1007.98	425.50	87182.84	96302.60	62817.16
129	1014.70	418.78	88197.54	96721.38	61802.46
130	1021.46	412.02	89219.00	97133.40	60781.00
131	1028.27	405.21	90247.27	97538.61	59752.73
132	1035.13	398.35	91282.40	97936.96	58717.60

133	1042.03	391.45	92324.43	98328.41	57675.57
134	1048.98	384.50	93373.41	98712.91	56626.59
135	1055.97	377.51	94429.38	99090.42	55570.62
136	1063.01	370.47	95492.39	99460.89	54507.61
137	1070.10	363.38	96562.49	99824.27	53437.51
138	1077.23	356.25	97639.72	100180.52	52360.28
139	1084.41	349.07	98724.13	100529.59	51275.87
140	1091.64	341.84	99815.77	100871.43	50184.23
141	1098.92	334.56	100914.69	101205.99	49085.31
142	1106.24	327.24	102020.93	101533.23	47979.07
143	1113.62	319.86	103134.55	101853.09	46865.45
144	1121.04	312.44	104255.59	102165.53	45744.41

145	1128.52	304.96	105384.11	102470.49	44615.89
146	1136.04	297.44	106520.15	102767.93	43479.85
147	1143.61	289.87	107663.76	103057.80	42336.24
148	1151.24	282.24	108815.00	103340.04	41185.00

149	1158.91	274.57	109973.91	103614.61	40026.09
150	1166.64	266.84	111140.55	103881.45	38859.45
151	1174.42	259.06	112314.97	104140.51	37685.03
152	1182.25	251.23	113497.22	104391.74	36502.78
153	1190.13	243.35	114687.35	104635.09	35312.65
154	1198.06	235.42	115885.41	104870.51	34114.59
155	1206.05	227.43	117091.46	105097.94	32908.54
156	1214.09	219.39	118305.55	105317.33	31694.45

157	1222.18	211.30	119527.73	105528.63	30472.27
158	1230.33	203.15	120758.06	105731.78	29241.94
159	1238.53	194.95	121996.59	105926.73	28003.41
160	1246.79	186.69	123243.38	106113.42	26756.62
161	1255.10	178.38	124498.48	106291.80	25501.52
162	1263.47	170.01	125761.95	106461.81	24238.05
163	1271.89	161.59	127033.84	106623.40	22966.16
164	1280.37	153.11	128314.21	106776.51	21685.79
165	1288.91	144.57	129603.12	106921.08	20396.88
166	1297.50	135.98	130900.62	107057.06	19099.38
167	1306.15	127.33	132206.77	107184.39	17793.23
168	1314.86	118.62	133521.63	107303.01	16478.37

169	1323.62	109.86	134845.25	107412.87	15154.75
170	1332.45	101.03	136177.70	107513.90	13822.30
171	1341.33	92.15	137519.03	107606.05	12480.97
172	1350.27	83.21	138869.30	107689.26	11130.70
173	1359.28	74.20	140228.58	107763.46	9771.42
174	1368.34	65.14	141596.92	107828.60	8403.08
175	1377.46	56.02	142974.38	107884.62	7025.62
176	1386.64	46.84	144361.02	107931.46	5638.98
177	1395.89	37.59	145756.91	107969.05	4243.09
178	1405.19	28.29	147162.10	107997.34	2837.90
179	1414.56	18.92	148576.66	108016.26	1423.34

| 180 | *1423.34 | 9.49 | 150000.00 | 108025.75 | 0.00 |

Now we will look at the balloon note with the seller. In this situation a seller can save you money. For example, you ask the seller to finance the property that you want to buy for eight years. You explain to him that you want to pay him less than prime but more than the going rate for a certificate of deposit. You will ask him to allow you to pay what the loan would be if it were amortized over 15 years but you want him to carry the loan for you for only eight years. At the end of eight years, a balloon note will be due, and he will no longer carry the mortgage either because you pay it off or because you take it to another lender to carry. Take a look:

Pmt	Principal	Interest	Cm Prin	Cm Int	Prin Bal
1	714.73	718.75	714.73	718.75	149285.27
2	718.15	715.33	1432.88	1434.08	148567.12
3	721.60	711.88	2154.48	2145.96	147845.52
4	725.05	708.43	2879.53	2854.39	147120.47
5	728.53	704.95	3608.06	3559.34	146391.94
6	732.02	701.46	4340.08	4260.80	145659.92
7	735.53	697.95	5075.61	4958.75	144924.39
8	739.05	694.43	5814.66	5653.18	144185.34
9	742.59	690.89	6557.25	6344.07	143442.75
10	746.15	687.33	7303.40	7031.40	142696.60
11	749.73	683.75	8053.13	7715.15	141946.87
12	753.32	680.16	8806.45	8395.31	141193.55
13	756.93	676.55	9563.38	9071.86	140436.62
14	760.55	672.93	10323.93	9744.79	139676.07
15	764.20	669.28	11088.13	10414.07	138911.87
16	767.86	665.62	11855.99	11079.69	138144.01
17	771.54	661.94	12627.53	11741.63	137372.47

18	775.24	658.24	13402.77	12399.87	136597.23
19	778.95	654.53	14181.72	13054.40	135818.28
20	782.68	650.80	14964.40	13705.20	135035.60
21	786.43	647.05	15750.83	14352.25	134249.17
22	790.20	643.28	16541.03	14995.53	133458.97
23	793.99	639.49	17335.02	15635.02	132664.98
24	797.79	635.69	18132.81	16270.71	131867.19

25	801.62	631.86	18934.43	16902.57	131065.57
26	805.46	628.02	19739.89	17530.59	130260.11
27	809.32	624.16	20549.21	18154.75	129450.79
28	813.19	620.29	21362.40	18775.04	128637.60
29	817.09	616.39	22179.49	19391.43	127820.51
30	821.01	612.47	23000.50	20003.90	126999.50
31	824.94	608.54	23825.44	20612.44	126174.56
32	828.89	604.59	24654.33	21217.03	125345.67
33	832.87	600.61	25487.20	21817.64	124512.80
34	836.86	596.62	26324.06	22414.26	123675.94
35	840.87	592.61	27164.93	23006.87	122835.07
36	844.90	588.58	28009.83	23595.45	121990.17

37	848.94	584.54	28858.77	24179.99	121141.23
38	853.01	580.47	29711.78	24760.46	120288.22
39	857.10	576.38	30568.88	25336.84	119431.12
40	861.21	572.27	31430.09	25909.11	118569.91
41	865.33	568.15	32295.42	26477.26	117704.58
42	869.48	564.00	33164.90	27041.26	116835.10
43	873.65	559.83	34038.55	27601.09	115961.45
44	877.83	555.65	34916.38	28156.74	115083.62
45	882.04	551.44	35798.42	28708.18	114201.58
46	886.26	547.22	36684.68	29255.40	113315.32
47	890.51	542.97	37575.19	29798.37	112424.81
48	894.78	538.70	38469.97	30337.07	111530.03

49	899.07	534.41	39369.04	30871.48	110630.96
50	903.37	530.11	40272.41	31401.59	109727.59
51	907.70	525.78	41180.11	31927.37	108819.89
52	912.05	521.43	42092.16	32448.80	107907.84
53	916.42	517.06	43008.58	32965.86	106991.42
54	920.81	512.67	43929.39	33478.53	106070.61
55	925.22	508.26	44854.61	33986.79	105145.39
56	929.66	503.82	45784.27	34490.61	104215.73
57	934.11	499.37	46718.38	34989.98	103281.62
58	938.59	494.89	47656.97	35484.87	102343.03
59	943.09	490.39	48600.06	35975.26	101399.94
60	947.61	485.87	49547.67	36461.13	100452.33

61	952.15	481.33	50499.82	36942.46	99500.18
62	956.71	476.77	51456.53	37419.23	98543.47
63	961.29	472.19	52417.82	37891.42	97582.18
64	965.90	467.58	53383.72	38359.00	96616.28
65	970.53	462.95	54354.25	38821.95	95645.75
66	975.18	458.30	55329.43	39280.25	94670.57
67	979.85	453.63	56309.28	39733.88	93690.72
68	984.55	448.93	57293.83	40182.81	92706.17
69	989.26	444.22	58283.09	40627.03	91716.91
70	994.00	439.48	59277.09	41066.51	90722.91
71	998.77	434.71	60275.86	41501.22	89724.14
72	1003.55	429.93	61279.41	41931.15	88720.59

73	1008.36	425.12	62287.77	42356.27	87712.23
74	1013.19	420.29	63300.96	42776.56	86699.04
75	1018.05	415.43	64319.01	43191.99	85680.99
76	1022.93	410.55	65341.94	43602.54	84658.06
77	1027.83	405.65	66369.77	44008.19	83630.23
78	1032.75	400.73	67402.52	44408.92	82597.48

79	1037.70	395.78	68440.22	44804.70	81559.78
80	1042.67	390.81	69482.89	45195.51	80517.11
81	1047.67	385.81	70530.56	45581.32	79469.44
82	1052.69	380.79	71583.25	45962.11	78416.75
83	1057.73	375.75	72640.98	46337.86	77359.02
84	1062.80	370.68	73703.78	46708.54	76296.22

85	1067.89	365.59	74771.67	47074.13	75228.33
86	1073.01	360.47	75844.68	47434.60	74155.32
87	1078.15	355.33	76922.83	47789.93	73077.17
88	1083.32	350.16	78006.15	48140.09	71993.85
89	1088.51	344.97	79094.66	48485.06	70905.34
90	1093.73	339.75	80188.39	48824.81	69811.61
91	1098.97	334.51	81287.36	49159.32	68712.64
92	1104.23	329.25	82391.59	49488.57	67608.41
93	1109.52	323.96	83501.11	49812.53	66498.89
94	1114.84	318.64	84615.95	50131.17	65384.05
95	1120.18	313.30	85736.13	50444.47	64263.87
96	1125.55	307.93	86861.68	50752.40	63138.32

At the end of the financing term, you will have paid only $201,054.96 and only $51,054.96 of that is in interest. Now, even though you owe a balloon payment of $63,440.88, you have saved a substantial amount of money because you have paid the seller only 5.75 percent interest compared to what you might have paid at the bank. In addition, over a period of eight years, you can save your money and draw interest from a bank as you wait for the loan to mature and the balloon note to be due. Further, you are able to keep your money available for other opportunities that may come along. Look at the worst case scenario and, for example, at the end of the eight years, you will need to finance the balloon payment through a traditional lender at 8 percent as the other two loans were financed. You do this for seven years.

This means you will pay an additional $19,618.36 in interest for a total interest paid of $70,673.32, saving you a remarkable $175,560.68 on a 30 year note and $37,533.08 on a traditional 15-year mortgage. See why the seller is often the best financier you can have?

Pmt	Principal	Interest	Cm Prin	Cm Int	Prin Bal
1	565.86	422.93	565.86	422.93	62874.14
2	569.63	419.16	1135.49	842.09	62304.51
3	573.43	415.36	1708.92	1257.45	61731.08
4	577.25	411.54	2286.17	1668.99	61153.83
5	581.10	407.69	2867.27	2076.68	60572.73
6	584.97	403.82	3452.24	2480.50	59987.76
7	588.87	399.92	4041.11	2880.42	59398.89
8	592.80	395.99	4633.91	3276.41	58806.09
9	596.75	392.04	5230.66	3668.45	58209.34
10	600.73	388.06	5831.39	4056.51	57608.61
11	604.73	384.06	6436.12	4440.57	57003.88
12	608.76	380.03	7044.88	4820.60	56395.12
13	612.82	375.97	7657.70	5196.57	55782.30
14	616.91	371.88	8274.61	5568.45	55165.39
15	621.02	367.77	8895.63	5936.22	54544.37
16	625.16	363.63	9520.79	6299.85	53919.21
17	629.33	359.46	10150.12	6659.31	53289.88
18	633.52	355.27	10783.64	7014.58	52656.36
19	637.75	351.04	11421.39	7365.62	52018.61
20	642.00	346.79	12063.39	7712.41	51376.61
21	646.28	342.51	12709.67	8054.92	50730.33
22	650.59	338.20	13360.26	8393.12	50079.74
23	654.93	333.86	14015.19	8726.98	49424.81
24	659.29	329.50	14674.48	9056.48	48765.52

25	663.69	325.10	15338.17	9381.58	48101.83
26	668.11	320.68	16006.28	9702.26	47433.72
27	672.57	316.22	16678.85	10018.48	46761.15
28	677.05	311.74	17355.90	10330.22	46084.10
29	681.56	307.23	18037.46	10637.45	45402.54
30	686.11	302.68	18723.57	10940.13	44716.43
31	690.68	298.11	19414.25	11238.24	44025.75
32	695.29	293.50	20109.54	11531.74	43330.46
33	699.92	288.87	20809.46	11820.61	42630.54
34	704.59	284.20	21514.05	12104.81	41925.95
35	709.28	279.51	22223.33	12384.32	41216.67
36	714.01	274.78	22937.34	12659.10	40502.66

37	718.77	270.02	23656.11	12929.12	39783.89
38	723.56	265.23	24379.67	13194.35	39060.33
39	728.39	260.40	25108.06	13454.75	38331.94
40	733.24	255.55	25841.30	13710.30	37598.70
41	738.13	250.66	26579.43	13960.96	36860.57
42	743.05	245.74	27322.48	14206.70	36117.52
43	748.01	240.78	28070.49	14447.48	35369.51
44	752.99	235.80	28823.48	14683.28	34616.52
45	758.01	230.78	29581.49	14914.06	33858.51
46	763.07	225.72	30344.56	15139.78	33095.44
47	768.15	220.64	31112.71	15360.42	32327.29
48	773.27	215.52	31885.98	15575.94	31554.02

49	778.43	210.36	32664.41	15786.30	30775.59
50	783.62	205.17	33448.03	15991.47	29991.97
51	788.84	199.95	34236.87	16191.42	29203.13
52	794.10	194.69	35030.97	16386.11	28409.03
53	799.40	189.39	35830.37	16575.50	27609.63
54	804.73	184.06	36635.10	16759.56	26804.90

55	810.09	178.70	37445.19	16938.26	25994.81
56	815.49	173.30	38260.68	17111.56	25179.32
57	820.93	167.86	39081.61	17279.42	24358.39
58	826.40	162.39	39908.01	17441.81	23531.99
59	831.91	156.88	40739.92	17598.69	22700.08
60	837.46	151.33	41577.38	17750.02	21862.62

61	843.04	145.75	42420.42	17895.77	21019.58
62	848.66	140.13	43269.08	18035.90	20170.92
63	854.32	134.47	44123.40	18170.37	19316.60
64	860.01	128.78	44983.41	18299.15	18456.59
65	865.75	123.04	45849.16	18422.19	17590.84
66	871.52	117.27	46720.68	18539.46	16719.32
67	877.33	111.46	47598.01	18650.92	15841.99
68	883.18	105.61	48481.19	18756.53	14958.81
69	889.06	99.73	49370.25	18856.26	14069.75
70	894.99	93.80	50265.24	18950.06	13174.76
71	900.96	87.83	51166.20	19037.89	12273.80
72	906.96	81.83	52073.16	19119.72	11366.84

73	913.01	75.78	52986.17	19195.50	10453.83
74	919.10	69.69	53905.27	19265.19	9534.73
75	925.23	63.56	54830.50	19328.75	8609.50
76	931.39	57.40	55761.89	19386.15	7678.11
77	937.60	51.19	56699.49	19437.34	6740.51
78	943.85	44.94	57643.34	19482.28	5796.66
79	950.15	38.64	58593.49	19520.92	4846.51
80	956.48	32.31	59549.97	19553.23	3890.03
81	962.86	25.93	60512.83	19579.16	2927.17
82	969.28	19.51	61482.11	19598.67	1957.89

| 83 | 975.74 | 13.05 | 62457.85 | 19611.72 | 982.15 |
| 84 | *982.15 | 6.55 | 63440.00 | 19618.27 | 0.00 |

Be creative no matter who helps you secure the financing for

FOOD FOR THOUGHT

I like lease-options but they are not for everyone. Not everyone would go to the trouble I will to find out about potential liens on a property and many people would fear rejection based on the terms I look for in a solid lease-option. Still, there are some personal reasons I prefer lease-options, and everyone has their own preferences. I have a friend who invests in Memphis but would never consider a lease-option or even financing. He will pay cash or he will do without. His wife, on the other hand will buy a lease-option when he is out of town and then insist he finance the property when he returns.

Let me tell you why I prefer lease-options and real estate options. Lease options offer a buyer the "option" to see if they like the property well enough to buy it. It is a "try before you really buy" thing but if you buy straight out, you do not have an out. You are stuck with a property you may not want because of yapping dogs next door or some other legitimate reason. In a lease-option, you are never locked into the deal. However, you will lose money if you do not buy, but often you can save a fortune with the try before you buy concept.

Options for consideration are beautiful. In my opinion, you should use leases with options to buy when you plan to buy and keep the property in your investment arsenal, and options should be used when you are just flipping properties and have no real interest in ever owning the property. You can get into an option contract for

CONTINUED as little as $1 and some believe even less if you can imagine that. Real estate options make it possible to be involved in a transaction where you can be a private party. In fact, the only people who need to know you ever owned interest in the property are the seller, the closing attorney, and the IRS.

the properties you want to buy, and always remember you will need to work out several different creative ways to finance your investment before you finally finance the entire purchase.

Where to Find the Money

There are so many places to find the money if you want to buy a property and yet not every loan is ideal for the property you are considering. Here, I want to talk about the overlapping mortgage. If you cannot find the money you need to finance your purchase anywhere else, often the best place to find it is in the equity you already have in an existing property. The overlapping mortgage can be used in seller-financing but you will use it with traditional lenders more often than with sellers. You are simply using two properties to stand good for the financing of one property.

Calling Off a Deal Going Bad

Having done your homework before you write up an offer to purchase, you may be able to avoid calling off a deal going bad right before it makes it to the closing table. But if not, you may learn about the downside to real estate investing the hard way.

Sure, it is just sickening to lose $500 or $1,000 but if you have good reasons to call off the deal in the middle of a contract, do so. By that I mean legitimate reasons such as a hand placed gently on a wall that crumbles in from termites, a sinking foundation, or a major roof leak you spot during the final walk-through.

If you are buying a home and the seller did not disclose everything to you in the early stages and you happen to catch a major flaw on the day of closing after the seller has moved, that is too bad for the seller. They will be more honest next time. Besides, since they will keep your binder, they can afford to move back into the house.

If you are in the middle of a real estate transaction and you catch something wrong, even if you lose your binder, do not close the deal. Moreover, WHY close the deal? Think about your overall investment. If you have been misled and you catch something while going through the final walk-through and know it is something that will cost you thousands of dollars down the road (such as a major roof leak), be willing to lose the $1,000 binder to avoid spending more later on.

This is one reason that both termite and home inspection reports are necessary before you close on any home. These inspections can prove to be more beneficial than the appraisal, and if you do not have one, later on you will wish you had. Home inspectors are generally forthcoming about roof and gutter problems and anything they note to be structurally incorrect about the home. It is well worth the money you pay to have an inspection done by a neutral party.

Chapter Eleven

The Undesirable Properties

I n real estate, you will hear about so-called undesirable properties. Whether there are such properties is up to the individual investor. Some people are inclined to believe that there are properties that are so undesirable they are to be avoided at all costs.

Take a look below at some of the properties you should avoid because these properties will never help you realize a quick profit and often it takes years for you to realize even a small return on your investment.

- Never buy a piece of property that has no city water and sewer.

- Restrictions are great in subdivisions but if they are too unrealistic for the average home owner to follow, then avoid investing in the property.

- As a new investor, never invest over your head no matter how much you are sure you can make.

- If you cannot secure a clean title, run!

I laugh whenever I have a client who tells me they are afraid to buy the property they are interested in buying. If I ask them why and they tell me it is because they have been to the courthouse, I smile and they look even more afraid until I assure them there is nothing to fear. All the liens will be washed away when they buy it. In fact, sometimes I will even pay for the title insurance for them just to give them peace of mind.

Real Estate Agent in Bristol, Tennessee

Dealing with Over-Financed Properties

America spends too much money. I know it and you know it. Knowing this, you should expect to run across the occasional property covered by liens when you are researching the property. America is covered in debt. As an investor, you really should expect to find liens on most of the properties, but do not panic when you do. They will disappear, in most cases, when the property is sold because all liens must be satisfied before a property is sold.

Too Many Liens Can Be Advantageous to the Buyer

If you are considering making an offer on a property that has been on the market for some time, go to the courthouse and research the property. Find out how much a seller paid for the property and then find out how much they owe on the property. If they owe a small amount on the property, you have little leverage, but think of the leverage you have if they do.

While you may perceive that you are taking advantage of the home owner covered in liens, you can also be their lifeline. If you offer them an amount that will satisfy their liens while offering them a way out from under a financial burden, you are their hero. Liens often cover a property that still has enough equity in it to give the homeowner some breathing room and a little bye-bye cash at the closing table. You can also get a great deal on a property with too many liens.

Working with Undesirables

The ripple effect of world-wide events and changing markets can help provide some guidance to the real estate investor looking for wise investments. Ignoring the events in the world outside the realm of real estate is detrimental and can cause investors to lose large sums of money. Savvy investors watch their local market and trends in real estate and world markets and events. For example, when foreign investors pull their capital away from U.S. companies and stocks, the Dow suffers, but in some areas the real estate market will seem stronger than ever. However, it would be safe for the investor who is constantly watching the markets to hold what they own and sell off anything they were planning to sell at a later date.

News of a failing economy will eventually touch the real estate industry and if smart investors are ready to capitalize on this, it will present great buying opportunities. When stocks take a slide, real estate investors who are conscious of the contrarian method of investing stand up and take notice, while the more conservative investors in real estate carry on with business as usual. Sometimes the outside factors touch them and sometimes they do not.

Natural disasters allow the contrarian investor to swing into action. Look at the coastal areas of Mississippi and the city of New Orleans. Some believe the areas will never recover. Some see opportunity. The contrarian investor sees a world of opportunity because of the devastation of the area that promises to come back stronger than ever before with smarter planning and better preparations for another disaster in the future. Others would not touch the area for any price. The contrarian investor views the unpredictable event of Hurricane Katrina as a devastating catastrophe but he also sees it as what it is—an opportunity. The areas most affected by Katrina will appeal to the strong investor who can walk in and offer a fair price for land and handy-man specials while helping to rebuild an area so crippled by the disaster. The contrarian investor is the crutch an area like Gulfport, Mississippi, needs. He or she will go into the area and help rebuild while making profits along the way. Even in the wake of a tragedy, this type of investor can profit while at the same time provide a means to an end for a stricken area.

If in doubt, look at the area of Biloxi, Mississippi. Before Hurricane Katrina, it was a booming town speckled with casinos and beautiful hotels. After Katrina, the casinos were in ruins. In the aftermath of Katrina, Biloxi will bounce back but they need strong investors to do so. The casinos are now able to move back, and in the devastation Legacy Condominiums begin to tower over the beach area with astronomical prices of over $400,000 per unit. This development is just the beginning. Investors are circling and they will profit as they revitalize the area into an economic giant again.

Smart investors take risks, but most are educated risks. They follow trends, collect data on other markets outside the real estate sector and know history repeats itself. In most cases, the real estate investor will diversify without realizing it. They hold rental and commercial properties and purchase homes with the intent to turn them quickly for a fast profit. Their portfolio often has properties in various locations with various means for bringing in income at different times of the month or the year.

Real estate is something real. It allows people to look at where their investment dollars are and more importantly, if bought as an investment tool, real estate can help investors generate profit either through re-sales or through ongoing residual monthly or even weekly income.

Damaged-by-Reputation

In the wake of Katrina as well as 9/11 and other catastrophes, one thing becomes apparent in real estate. Smart investors sell when the masses are convinced it is all right to buy again. The investors sell when the general public becomes interested in the area again, but the smart investor never lost interest because they viewed the area with dollar signs in their eyes.

The same holds true for local investors throughout the world. In small town America, a real estate agent takes a couple through a REO (real estate owned) property owned by a local bank. She slowly opens a bedroom door as if she is expecting a big dog to attack her and when she does, she still sees in the sunlight there are blood stains on the wall. She explains to the couple that the reason the bank is taking sealed bids on the house is because the home was going into foreclosure because of the murder that took place in the home. No survivors were apparent and the bank reclaimed the property. The investors seem unbothered by the events, as she describes the situation, because they had already heard about it within the community. They place a bid on the home which is about 50 percent of the home's true value and they feel confident they will win the bid.

Damaged-by-reputation is what I like to call the damaged homes no one else wants. These homes are usually only damaged-by-reputation for a short time. An investor can go into the home, gut it if necessary, return it to the market at the appropriate time, and make a fortune on it. Even if people do not forget, it is amazing what a new look can do for a home with fresh paint, new appliances, and flooring.

The home of Nicole Brown Simpson is an example of how damaged-by-reputation homes are often profitable for investors. The Simpson family sold Nicole's condominium for around $500,000 which was reportedly $200,000 less than she paid for it according to 20/20 and ABC News. The condominium re-entered the marketplace for $1.8 million asking price recently, proving the stigma is either lifted or unimportant to the person asking the $1.8 million and to those who will buy it.

When you see a property which has been damaged by an unforgettable or horrific crime, the reputation is typically at a stalemate in the beginning. This enables the investor who can buy these properties to gain huge profits. The best buying situation for these buyers is to purchase the property as soon as it goes on the market for sale because it is during this time that a home owner will not know the value of the property. The perceived value at the time is generally close to zero. Obviously, there will be a price for taking the property off of the current owner's hands but it will be low. Typically, an investor can go in and make some changes and improvements then return it to the market when the stigma wears down. Will the stigma wear off? Probably not but people forget and sooner or later it will become just another house and regain its value.

Chapter Twelve

How to Find the Money You Need

If a buyer is ready to buy and a seller is ready to let the buyer take the property off his hands, nothing will stand in the way of meeting in the middle somewhere unless of course, money is a factor. This is the point when one or both parties may decide that being creative would not hurt the chances of coming to a mutual decision.

Where to Find the Money

In most cases, investors know where their money is coming from when they decide to write an offer to purchase. They know how much they need and they know how they will finance their purchase. An investor looking for creative financing will use one of the following measures:

1. Seller-financing through a Purchase-Money Mortgage

2. Second Mortgage

3. Assumable Mortgage

4. Private Lenders

5. Wraparound Mortgages

6. Overlapping Mortgage

7. Equity Sharing

8. Lease with Option to Buy

9. Rent-to-Own

In seller-financing, a buyer and seller can move quickly toward an amicable closing if the seller understands how seller-financing works. It is the investor's job to assure the seller of timely payments and to remind the seller of the interest he or she is going to be earning. Buyers find sellers who are willing to finance them because they know the value in owner-financing, they know the interest money they will make, and they understand that the interest earned on a purchase-money mortgage is better than the money they can hope to make in the stock market or in any other investment. It is solid and secured by the real estate.

With a good real estate attorney or title company handling the closing of a seller financed transaction, everything should move along without any problems. As a buyer with a seller carrying the mortgage, you need to understand the seller will probably want to see payment receipts for the insurance premiums on the property. Understand, this is something they will ask for or they may place a clause in the contract about insurance. If you have questions, always check with the agent or attorney before signing your closing documents.

Another form of creatively financing your investment can be through the use of second mortgages. This is one of the main ways real estate investors will finance their properties. They may get help on the first property through seller-financing, pay it off, take a mortgage against it to buy another home, pay that down, and take a second to buy home number three. It happens all the time. Using a traditional lender is common for second mortgages. However, second mortgages can also be used in other ways with the seller.

Very often a seller will take back a second mortgage to help the buyer with closing costs and the down payment. When used creatively, the seller will pay the closing costs and provide 10 percent to 20 percent of the purchase price for the down payment. It can allow the investor to purchase the home without any money down and without any of their own cash.

Is there any better way to purchase real estate? Yes, through the assumable loan—something only offered only on select properties. Many VA and FHA loans are assumable but it is important to remember the seller does not get to decide who assumes their loan. Typically, a new loan process will be started and those who qualify on their own are able to assume the loan with few additional fees. In most cases, qualifying for an assumable mortgage is much easier than through traditional financing.

Private lenders are another source for investors to consider when financing their properties. If you are interested in buying multiple properties using private lenders, it is a good idea to get recommendations from real estate agents. In years past, many private lenders were to be avoided because of their collection tactics and quick move to foreclosure because a late payment, but now things are different. You should be able to use a private lender with the same terms you would typically find at a bank or other lending institution with some payment flexibility but at a higher interest rate.

Another creative way to finance your purchase is through the use of an all-inclusive mortgage also referred to as the wrap-around mortgage. If the seller is open to the all-inclusive mortgage it is a viable way for an investor to buy. What happens in this case is the buyer and seller work together by wrapping the current mortgage around the new financing. This is generally not a favorable way to invest.

One commonly used mortgage is called the overlapping mortgage, a favorite of investors. In the case of the overlapping mortgage, two properties are used. Often, it will be considered favorable by the lender because under most circumstances one property shows a fair amount of equity built into the real estate. Overlapping mortgages are used mostly in farm deals and land deals.

Investors will often turn to other investors when they first start out in real estate because the more experienced investors are the go-to source for learning more about the business. However, if you go to a savvy business-minded investor as a mentor, be prepared to share equity in the property you want the investor to help you finance.

Here is how equity sharing works. (Keep in mind; if you are using an investor because of your bad credit or no credit, you are at their mercy so try to avoid any snags.) Equity sharing works like a partnership and it is a bad deal in my opinion if you are an investor buying and selling property for profit. There are lots of ways for the equity sharing to work out. Essentially what will happen is the investor will put up the money for the purchase of the home and they will want to share in the equity. A contract will be written to protect the interest of both parties and when the property sells, the investors split the appreciated value of the home.

In equity sharing, both investors need to protect their interests. Things such as who owns what if someone dies should be discussed as well as what home improvements would be split and what improvements would be the sole responsibility of the investor borrowing the money.

As an investor, you want to avoid using other investors' money if they want more than their interest money. If they also want a large percentage of profit when the time comes to sell, you simply will not profit after you subtract expenses and what you have paid into the house.

Investors can also enter into a lease-option with an option to buy the property they want to own and a rent-to-own agreement. The rent-to-own agreement is not a good choice for the investor because the landlord who offers the rent-to-own is not keen on having another investor rent and then sublet to someone else, but in some circumstances, this procedure can work.

Lease options are fantastic investor tools. If you work them out to your benefit, a lease-option is the best way to invest in many cases. For instance, if you are facing a divorce and you want to start building equity in something but you do not want to have your name in your local newspaper as a new homeowner or recorded on the deed, a lease is a perfect solution. In many cases, a lease-option is just a more refined way to rent-to-own when you can lease for a longer term.

Getting Money Out of Your 401(k)

As a realtor, I worked with several investors, new home owners, or first-time buyers. Many times I watched young couples dig into their 401(k) to pay their down payments and closing costs. I can tell you doing this is a long drawn-out experience. If you are going to be using your 401(k) for anything, find out how long it takes to obtain disbursements from your 401(k) and see what you can do to speed things up in the initial stages so that you are not the holdup.

A 401(k) is an excellent tool to use for your real estate transactions. Talk to a mortgage lending officer about using your 401(k) before you dive right into it and find out everything you need to know before you use proceeds from it.

Using Your Self-Directed IRA

Often, investors become so wrapped up in the traditional way of finding money for their real estate purchases, they forget to notice where they have money available to use. An IRA retirement plan is one such place. A self-directed IRA can allow investors the opportunity to use some of their funds to invest in real estate.

Years ago many people thought the only holdings they could have in their IRA account were stocks, bonds, and mutual funds, but now investors know they can just as easily hold real estate in their IRA. In fact, as an investor, it is smart business to have real property in your IRA portfolio.

A Note About Short-Term Loans

Short-term loans can become risky if a quick decision is made about securing it with little buyer appeal and stiff terms. Beware of short-term loans that are amortized over 30 years to give you a payment you can afford right now especially if a quick fix on your credit will not do the trick at the end of the term of the loan. Take a look at the example below.

Connie wants more than she and Tom can afford. He wants more than they can afford too but finds a way, he thinks, to put Connie in her dream home. They meet a builder who has "sat" on a house too long; they explain to him their current financial situation, and the builder offers to owner-finance the home to them for five years with a balloon at the end of that time. The house is priced at $250,000. Feeling generous, the builder decides a 7 percent interest rate is fair considering the couple has no credit history. At the end of the term, as you will note below, the couple will have a balloon note of $284,463.16 because the builder offers to let the couple move in for $1,000 a month which does not even pay the interest on the money they are going to borrow for the home.

Pmt	Principal	Interest	Cm Prin	Cm Int	Prin Bal
1	-458.33	1458.33	-458.33	1458.33	250458.33
2	-461.01	1461.01	-919.34	2919.34	250919.34
3	-463.70	1463.70	-1383.04	4383.04	251383.04
4	-466.40	1466.40	-1849.44	5849.44	251849.44
5	-469.12	1469.12	-2318.56	7318.56	252318.56
6	-471.86	1471.86	-2790.42	8790.42	252790.42
7	-474.61	1474.61	-3265.03	10265.03	253265.03
8	-477.38	1477.38	-3742.41	11742.41	253742.41
9	-480.16	1480.16	-4222.57	13222.57	254222.57

10	-482.96	1482.96	-4705.53	14705.53	254705.53
11	-485.78	1485.78	-5191.31	16191.31	255191.31
12	-488.62	1488.62	-5679.93	17679.93	255679.93

13	-491.47	1491.47	-6171.40	19171.40	256171.40
14	-494.33	1494.33	-6665.73	20665.73	256665.73
15	-497.22	1497.22	-7162.95	22162.95	257162.95
16	-500.12	1500.12	-7663.07	23663.07	257663.07
17	-503.03	1503.03	-8166.10	25166.10	258166.10
18	-505.97	1505.97	-8672.07	26672.07	258672.07
19	-508.92	1508.92	-9180.99	28180.99	259180.99
20	-511.89	1511.89	-9692.88	29692.88	259692.88
21	-514.88	1514.88	-10207.76	31207.76	260207.76
22	-517.88	1517.88	-10725.64	32725.64	260725.64
23	-520.90	1520.90	-11246.54	34246.54	261246.54
24	-523.94	1523.94	-11770.48	35770.48	261770.48

25	-526.99	1526.99	-12297.47	37297.47	262297.47
26	-530.07	1530.07	-12827.54	38827.54	262827.54
27	-533.16	1533.16	-13360.70	40360.70	263360.70
28	-536.27	1536.27	-13896.97	41896.97	263896.97
29	-539.40	1539.40	-14436.37	43436.37	264436.37
30	-542.55	1542.55	-14978.92	44978.92	264978.92
31	-545.71	1545.71	-15524.63	46524.63	265524.63
32	-548.89	1548.89	-16073.52	48073.52	266073.52
33	-552.10	1552.10	-16625.62	49625.62	266625.62
34	-555.32	1555.32	-17180.94	51180.94	267180.94
35	-558.56	1558.56	-17739.50	52739.50	267739.50
36	-561.81	1561.81	-18301.31	54301.31	268301.31
37	-565.09	1565.09	-18866.40	55866.40	268866.40
38	-568.39	1568.39	-19434.79	57434.79	269434.79
39	-571.70	1571.70	-20006.49	59006.49	270006.49

40	-575.04	1575.04	-20581.53	60581.53	270581.53
41	-578.39	1578.39	-21159.92	62159.92	271159.92
42	-581.77	1581.77	-21741.69	63741.69	271741.69
43	-585.16	1585.16	-22326.85	65326.85	272326.85
44	-588.57	1588.57	-22915.42	66915.42	272915.42
45	-592.01	1592.01	-23507.43	68507.43	273507.43
46	-595.46	1595.46	-24102.89	70102.89	274102.89
47	-598.93	1598.93	-24701.82	71701.82	274701.82
48	-602.43	1602.43	-25304.25	73304.25	275304.25

49	-605.94	1605.94	-25910.19	74910.19	275910.19
50	-609.48	1609.48	-26519.67	76519.67	276519.67
51	-613.03	1613.03	-27132.70	78132.70	277132.70
52	-616.61	1616.61	-27749.31	79749.31	277749.31
53	-620.20	1620.20	-28369.51	81369.51	278369.51
54	-623.82	1623.82	-28993.33	82993.33	278993.33
55	-627.46	1627.46	-29620.79	84620.79	279620.79
56	-631.12	1631.12	-30251.91	86251.91	280251.91
57	-634.80	1634.80	-30886.71	87886.71	280886.71
58	-638.51	1638.51	-31525.22	89525.22	281525.22
59	-642.23	1642.23	-32167.45	91167.45	282167.45
60	-645.98	1645.98	-32813.43	92813.43	282813.43

| 61 | *282813.43 | 1649.75 | 250000.00 | 94463.18 | -0.00 |

Take the same figure of $250,000 and spread it over five years with a more realistic payment of $1,800 per month. At the end of five years, the young couple will still face a balloon payment of $226,854.74, and chances are they will not be in any better shape financially to afford the home in five years than they are the day they move in.

Pmt	Principal	Interest	Cm Prin	Cm Int	Prin Bal
1	341.67	1458.33	341.67	1458.33	249658.33
2	343.66	1456.34	685.33	2914.67	249314.67
3	345.66	1454.34	1030.99	4369.01	248969.01
4	347.68	1452.32	1378.67	5821.33	248621.33
5	349.71	1450.29	1728.38	7271.62	248271.62
6	351.75	1448.25	2080.13	8719.87	247919.87
7	353.80	1446.20	2433.93	10166.07	247566.07
8	355.86	1444.14	2789.79	11610.21	247210.21
9	357.94	1442.06	3147.73	13052.27	246852.27
10	360.03	1439.97	3507.76	14492.24	246492.24
11	362.13	1437.87	3869.89	15930.11	246130.11
12	364.24	1435.76	4234.13	17365.87	245765.87
13	366.37	1433.63	4600.50	18799.50	245399.50
14	368.50	1431.50	4969.00	20231.00	245031.00
15	370.65	1429.35	5339.65	21660.35	244660.35
16	372.81	1427.19	5712.46	23087.54	244287.54
17	374.99	1425.01	6087.45	24512.55	243912.55
18	377.18	1422.82	6464.63	25935.37	243535.37
19	379.38	1420.62	6844.01	27355.99	243155.99
20	381.59	1418.41	7225.60	28774.40	242774.40
21	383.82	1416.18	7609.42	30190.58	242390.58
22	386.05	1413.95	7995.47	31604.53	242004.53
23	388.31	1411.69	8383.78	33016.22	241616.22
24	390.57	1409.43	8774.35	34425.65	241225.65
25	392.85	1407.15	9167.20	35832.80	240832.80
26	395.14	1404.86	9562.34	37237.66	240437.66
27	397.45	1402.55	9959.79	38640.21	240040.21
28	399.77	1400.23	10359.56	40040.44	239640.44
29	402.10	1397.90	10761.66	41438.34	239238.34
30	404.44	1395.56	11166.10	42833.90	238833.90

31	406.80	1393.20	11572.90	44227.10	238427.10
32	409.18	1390.82	11982.08	45617.92	238017.92
33	411.56	1388.44	12393.64	47006.36	237606.36
34	413.96	1386.04	12807.60	48392.40	237192.40
35	416.38	1383.62	13223.98	49776.02	236776.02
36	418.81	1381.19	13642.79	51157.21	236357.21

37	421.25	1378.75	14064.04	52535.96	235935.96
38	423.71	1376.29	14487.75	53912.25	235512.25
39	426.18	1373.82	14913.93	55286.07	235086.07
40	428.66	1371.34	15342.59	56657.41	234657.41
41	431.17	1368.83	15773.76	58026.24	234226.24
42	433.68	1366.32	16207.44	59392.56	233792.56
43	436.21	1363.79	16643.65	60756.35	233356.35
44	438.75	1361.25	17082.40	62117.60	232917.60
45	441.31	1358.69	17523.71	63476.29	232476.29
46	443.89	1356.11	17967.60	64832.40	232032.40
47	446.48	1353.52	18414.08	66185.92	231585.92
48	449.08	1350.92	18863.16	67536.84	231136.84

49	451.70	1348.30	19314.86	68885.14	230685.14
50	454.34	1345.66	19769.20	70230.80	230230.80
51	456.99	1343.01	20226.19	71573.81	229773.81
52	459.65	1340.35	20685.84	72914.16	229314.16
53	462.33	1337.67	21148.17	74251.83	228851.83
54	465.03	1334.97	21613.20	75586.80	228386.80
55	467.74	1332.26	22080.94	76919.06	227919.06
56	470.47	1329.53	22551.41	78248.59	227448.59
57	473.22	1326.78	23024.63	79575.37	226975.37
58	475.98	1324.02	23500.61	80899.39	226499.39
59	478.75	1321.25	23979.36	82220.64	226020.64
60	481.55	1318.45	24460.91	83539.09	225539.09

The problem with short-term notes is that they are often a quick fix to get someone into a home they truly cannot afford. Take that $250,000 home above and amortize it over 30 years at 7 percent interest and you will see a payment of $1,663.26. Considering the payment is $2,900 per month before taxes, a person making $35,000 a year cannot afford a $250,000 home based on one income alone.

Pmt	Principal	Interest	Cm Prin	Cm Int	Prin Bal
1	204.93	1458.33	204.93	1458.33	249795.07
2	206.12	1457.14	411.05	2915.47	249588.95
3	207.32	1455.94	618.37	4371.41	249381.63
4	208.53	1454.73	826.90	5826.14	249173.10
5	209.75	1453.51	1036.65	7279.65	248963.35
6	210.97	1452.29	1247.62	8731.94	248752.38
7	212.20	1451.06	1459.82	10183.00	248540.18
8	213.44	1449.82	1673.26	11632.82	248326.74
9	214.69	1448.57	1887.95	13081.39	248112.05
10	215.94	1447.32	2103.89	14528.71	247896.11
11	217.20	1446.06	2321.09	15974.77	247678.91
12	218.47	1444.79	2539.56	17419.56	247460.44

Pmt	Principal	Interest	Cm Prin	Cm Int	Prin Bal
13	219.74	1443.52	2759.30	18863.08	247240.70
14	221.02	1442.24	2980.32	20305.32	247019.68
15	222.31	1440.95	3202.63	21746.27	246797.37
16	223.61	1439.65	3426.24	23185.92	246573.76
17	224.91	1438.35	3651.15	24624.27	246348.85
18	226.23	1437.03	3877.38	26061.30	246122.62
19	227.54	1435.72	4104.92	27497.02	245895.08
20	228.87	1434.39	4333.79	28931.41	245666.21
21	230.21	1433.05	4564.00	30364.46	245436.00
22	231.55	1431.71	4795.55	31796.17	245204.45
23	232.90	1430.36	5028.45	33226.53	244971.55

24	234.26	1429.00	5262.71	34655.53	244737.29

25	235.63	1427.63	5498.34	36083.16	244501.66
26	237.00	1426.26	5735.34	37509.42	244264.66
27	238.38	1424.88	5973.72	38934.30	244026.28
28	239.77	1423.49	6213.49	40357.79	243786.51
29	241.17	1422.09	6454.66	41779.88	243545.34
30	242.58	1420.68	6697.24	43200.56	243302.76
31	243.99	1419.27	6941.23	44619.83	243058.77
32	245.42	1417.84	7186.65	46037.67	242813.35
33	246.85	1416.41	7433.50	47454.08	242566.50
34	248.29	1414.97	7681.79	48869.05	242318.21
35	249.74	1413.52	7931.53	50282.57	242068.47
36	251.19	1412.07	8182.72	51694.64	241817.28

37	252.66	1410.60	8435.38	53105.24	241564.62
38	254.13	1409.13	8689.51	54514.37	241310.49
39	255.62	1407.64	8945.13	55922.01	241054.87
40	257.11	1406.15	9202.24	57328.16	240797.76
41	258.61	1404.65	9460.85	58732.81	240539.15
42	260.11	1403.15	9720.96	60135.96	240279.04
43	261.63	1401.63	9982.59	61537.59	240017.41
44	263.16	1400.10	10245.75	62937.69	239754.25
45	264.69	1398.57	10510.44	64336.26	239489.56
46	266.24	1397.02	10776.68	65733.28	239223.32
47	267.79	1395.47	11044.47	67128.75	238955.53
48	269.35	1393.91	11313.82	68522.66	238686.18

49	270.92	1392.34	11584.74	69915.00	238415.26
50	272.50	1390.76	11857.24	71305.76	238142.76
51	274.09	1389.17	12131.33	72694.93	237868.67
52	275.69	1387.57	12407.02	74082.50	237592.98
53	277.30	1385.96	12684.32	75468.46	237315.68

54	278.92	1384.34	12963.24	76852.80	237036.76
55	280.55	1382.71	13243.79	78235.51	236756.21
56	282.18	1381.08	13525.97	79616.59	236474.03
57	283.83	1379.43	13809.80	80996.02	236190.20
58	285.48	1377.78	14095.28	82373.80	235904.72
59	287.15	1376.11	14382.43	83749.91	235617.57
60	288.82	1374.44	14671.25	85124.35	235328.75

61	290.51	1372.75	14961.76	86497.10	235038.24
62	292.20	1371.06	15253.96	87868.16	234746.04
63	293.91	1369.35	15547.87	89237.51	234452.13
64	295.62	1367.64	15843.49	90605.15	234156.51
65	297.35	1365.91	16140.84	91971.06	233859.16
66	299.08	1364.18	16439.92	93335.24	233560.08
67	300.83	1362.43	16740.75	94697.67	233259.25
68	302.58	1360.68	17043.33	96058.35	232956.67
69	304.35	1358.91	17347.68	97417.26	232652.32
70	306.12	1357.14	17653.80	98774.40	232346.20
71	307.91	1355.35	17961.71	100129.75	232038.29
72	309.70	1353.56	18271.41	101483.31	231728.59

73	311.51	1351.75	18582.92	102835.06	231417.08
74	313.33	1349.93	18896.25	104184.99	231103.75
75	315.15	1348.11	19211.40	105533.10	230788.60
76	316.99	1346.27	19528.39	106879.37	230471.61
77	318.84	1344.42	19847.23	108223.79	230152.77
78	320.70	1342.56	20167.93	109566.35	229832.07
79	322.57	1340.69	20490.50	110907.04	229509.50
80	324.45	1338.81	20814.95	112245.85	229185.05
81	326.35	1336.91	21141.30	113582.76	228858.70
82	328.25	1335.01	21469.55	114917.77	228530.45
83	330.17	1333.09	21799.72	116250.86	228200.28
84	332.09	1331.17	22131.81	117582.03	227868.19

85	334.03	1329.23	22465.84	118911.26	227534.16
86	335.98	1327.28	22801.82	120238.54	227198.18
87	337.94	1325.32	23139.76	121563.86	226860.24
88	339.91	1323.35	23479.67	122887.21	226520.33
89	341.89	1321.37	23821.56	124208.58	226178.44
90	343.89	1319.37	24165.45	125527.95	225834.55
91	345.89	1317.37	24511.34	126845.32	225488.66
92	347.91	1315.35	24859.25	128160.67	225140.75
93	349.94	1313.32	25209.19	129473.99	224790.81
94	351.98	1311.28	25561.17	130785.27	224438.83
95	354.03	1309.23	25915.20	132094.50	224084.80
96	356.10	1307.16	26271.30	133401.66	223728.70

97	358.18	1305.08	26629.48	134706.74	223370.52
98	360.27	1302.99	26989.75	136009.73	223010.25
99	362.37	1300.89	27352.12	137310.62	222647.88
100	364.48	1298.78	27716.60	138609.40	222283.40
101	366.61	1296.65	28083.21	139906.05	221916.79
102	368.75	1294.51	28451.96	141200.56	221548.04
103	370.90	1292.36	28822.86	142492.92	221177.14
104	373.06	1290.20	29195.92	143783.12	220804.08
105	375.24	1288.02	29571.16	145071.14	220428.84
106	377.43	1285.83	29948.59	146356.97	220051.41
107	379.63	1283.63	30328.22	147640.60	219671.78
108	381.84	1281.42	30710.06	148922.02	219289.94

109	384.07	1279.19	31094.13	150201.21	218905.87
110	386.31	1276.95	31480.44	151478.16	218519.56
111	388.56	1274.70	31869.00	152752.86	218131.00
112	390.83	1272.43	32259.83	154025.29	217740.17
113	393.11	1270.15	32652.94	155295.44	217347.06
114	395.40	1267.86	33048.34	156563.30	216951.66
115	397.71	1265.55	33446.05	157828.85	216553.95

116	400.03	1263.23	33846.08	159092.08	216153.92
117	402.36	1260.90	34248.44	160352.98	215751.56
118	404.71	1258.55	34653.15	161611.53	215346.85
119	407.07	1256.19	35060.22	162867.72	214939.78
120	409.44	1253.82	35469.66	164121.54	214530.34

121	411.83	1251.43	35881.49	165372.97	214118.51
122	414.24	1249.02	36295.73	166621.99	213704.27
123	416.65	1246.61	36712.38	167868.60	213287.62
124	419.08	1244.18	37131.46	169112.78	212868.54
125	421.53	1241.73	37552.99	170354.51	212447.01
126	423.99	1239.27	37976.98	171593.78	212023.02
127	426.46	1236.80	38403.44	172830.58	211596.56
128	428.95	1234.31	38832.39	174064.89	211167.61
129	431.45	1231.81	39263.84	175296.70	210736.16
130	433.97	1229.29	39697.81	176525.99	210302.19
131	436.50	1226.76	40134.31	177752.75	209865.69
132	439.04	1224.22	40573.35	178976.97	209426.65

133	441.60	1221.66	41014.95	180198.63	208985.05
134	444.18	1219.08	41459.13	181417.71	208540.87
135	446.77	1216.49	41905.90	182634.20	208094.10
136	449.38	1213.88	42355.28	183848.08	207644.72
137	452.00	1211.26	42807.28	185059.34	207192.72
138	454.64	1208.62	43261.92	186267.96	206738.08
139	457.29	1205.97	43719.21	187473.93	206280.79
140	459.96	1203.30	44179.17	188677.23	205820.83
141	462.64	1200.62	44641.81	189877.85	205358.19
142	465.34	1197.92	45107.15	191075.77	204892.85
143	468.05	1195.21	45575.20	192270.98	204424.80
144	470.78	1192.48	46045.98	193463.46	203954.02

145	473.53	1189.73	46519.51	194653.19	203480.49

146	476.29	1186.97	46995.80	195840.16	203004.20
147	479.07	1184.19	47474.87	197024.35	202525.13
148	481.86	1181.40	47956.73	198205.75	202043.27
149	484.67	1178.59	48441.40	199384.34	201558.60
150	487.50	1175.76	48928.90	200560.10	201071.10
151	490.35	1172.91	49419.25	201733.01	200580.75
152	493.21	1170.05	49912.46	202903.06	200087.54
153	496.08	1167.18	50408.54	204070.24	199591.46
154	498.98	1164.28	50907.52	205234.52	199092.48
155	501.89	1161.37	51409.41	206395.89	198590.59
156	504.81	1158.45	51914.22	207554.34	198085.78

157	507.76	1155.50	52421.98	208709.84	197578.02
158	510.72	1152.54	52932.70	209862.38	197067.30
159	513.70	1149.56	53446.40	211011.94	196553.60
160	516.70	1146.56	53963.10	212158.50	196036.90
161	519.71	1143.55	54482.81	213302.05	195517.19
162	522.74	1140.52	55005.55	214442.57	194994.45
163	525.79	1137.47	55531.34	215580.04	194468.66
164	528.86	1134.40	56060.20	216714.44	193939.80
165	531.94	1131.32	56592.14	217845.76	193407.86
166	535.05	1128.21	57127.19	218973.97	192872.81
167	538.17	1125.09	57665.36	220099.06	192334.64
168	541.31	1121.95	58206.67	221221.01	191793.33

169	544.47	1118.79	58751.14	222339.80	191248.86
170	547.64	1115.62	59298.78	223455.42	190701.22
171	550.84	1112.42	59849.62	224567.84	190150.38
172	554.05	1109.21	60403.67	225677.05	189596.33
173	557.28	1105.98	60960.95	226783.03	189039.05
174	560.53	1102.73	61521.48	227885.76	188478.52
175	563.80	1099.46	62085.28	228985.22	187914.72

176	567.09	1096.17	62652.37	230081.39	187347.63
177	570.40	1092.86	63222.77	231174.25	186777.23
178	573.73	1089.53	63796.50	232263.78	186203.50
179	577.07	1086.19	64373.57	233349.97	185626.43
180	580.44	1082.82	64954.01	234432.79	185045.99

181	583.83	1079.43	65537.84	235512.22	184462.16
182	587.23	1076.03	66125.07	236588.25	183874.93
183	590.66	1072.60	66715.73	237660.85	183284.27
184	594.10	1069.16	67309.83	238730.01	182690.17
185	597.57	1065.69	67907.40	239795.70	182092.60
186	601.05	1062.21	68508.45	240857.91	181491.55
187	604.56	1058.70	69113.01	241916.61	180886.99
188	608.09	1055.17	69721.10	242971.78	180278.90
189	611.63	1051.63	70332.73	244023.41	179667.27
190	615.20	1048.06	70947.93	245071.47	179052.07
191	618.79	1044.47	71566.72	246115.94	178433.28
192	622.40	1040.86	72189.12	247156.80	177810.88

193	626.03	1037.23	72815.15	248194.03	177184.85
194	629.68	1033.58	73444.83	249227.61	176555.17
195	633.35	1029.91	74078.18	250257.52	175921.82
196	637.05	1026.21	74715.23	251283.73	175284.77
197	640.77	1022.49	75356.00	252306.22	174644.00
198	644.50	1018.76	76000.50	253324.98	173999.50
199	648.26	1015.00	76648.76	254339.98	173351.24
200	652.04	1011.22	77300.80	255351.20	172699.20
201	655.85	1007.41	77956.65	256358.61	172043.35
202	659.67	1003.59	78616.32	257362.20	171383.68
203	663.52	999.74	79279.84	258361.94	170720.16
204	667.39	995.87	79947.23	259357.81	170052.77

205	671.29	991.97	80618.52	260349.78	169381.48

206	675.20	988.06	81293.72	261337.84	168706.28
207	679.14	984.12	81972.86	262321.96	168027.14
208	683.10	980.16	82655.96	263302.12	167344.04
209	687.09	976.17	83343.05	264278.29	166656.95
210	691.09	972.17	84034.14	265250.46	165965.86
211	695.13	968.13	84729.27	266218.59	165270.73
212	699.18	964.08	85428.45	267182.67	164571.55
213	703.26	960.00	86131.71	268142.67	163868.29
214	707.36	955.90	86839.07	269098.57	163160.93
215	711.49	951.77	87550.56	270050.34	162449.44
216	715.64	947.62	88266.20	270997.96	161733.80

217	719.81	943.45	88986.01	271941.41	161013.99
218	724.01	939.25	89710.02	272880.66	160289.98
219	728.24	935.02	90438.26	273815.68	159561.74
220	732.48	930.78	91170.74	274746.46	158829.26
221	736.76	926.50	91907.50	275672.96	158092.50
222	741.05	922.21	92648.55	276595.17	157351.45
223	745.38	917.88	93393.93	277513.05	156606.07
224	749.72	913.54	94143.65	278426.59	155856.35
225	754.10	909.16	94897.75	279335.75	155102.25
226	758.50	904.76	95656.25	280240.51	154343.75
227	762.92	900.34	96419.17	281140.85	153580.83
228	767.37	895.89	97186.54	282036.74	152813.46

229	771.85	891.41	97958.39	282928.15	152041.61
230	776.35	886.91	98734.74	283815.06	151265.26
231	780.88	882.38	99515.62	284697.44	150484.38
232	785.43	877.83	100301.05	285575.27	149698.95
233	790.02	873.24	101091.07	286448.51	148908.93
234	794.62	868.64	101885.69	287317.15	148114.31
235	799.26	864.00	102684.95	288181.15	147315.05
236	803.92	859.34	103488.87	289040.49	146511.13

237	808.61	854.65	104297.48	289895.14	145702.52
238	813.33	849.93	105110.81	290745.07	144889.19
239	818.07	845.19	105928.88	291590.26	144071.12
240	822.85	840.41	106751.73	292430.67	143248.27

241	827.65	835.61	107579.38	293266.28	142420.62
242	832.47	830.79	108411.85	294097.07	141588.15
243	837.33	825.93	109249.18	294923.00	140750.82
244	842.21	821.05	110091.39	295744.05	139908.61
245	847.13	816.13	110938.52	296560.18	139061.48
246	852.07	811.19	111790.59	297371.37	138209.41
247	857.04	806.22	112647.63	298177.59	137352.37
248	862.04	801.22	113509.67	298978.81	136490.33
249	867.07	796.19	114376.74	299775.00	135623.26
250	872.12	791.14	115248.86	300566.14	134751.14
251	877.21	786.05	116126.07	301352.19	133873.93
252	882.33	780.93	117008.40	302133.12	132991.60

253	887.48	775.78	117895.88	302908.90	132104.12
254	892.65	770.61	118788.53	303679.51	131211.47
255	897.86	765.40	119686.39	304444.91	130313.61
256	903.10	760.16	120589.49	305205.07	129410.51
257	908.37	754.89	121497.86	305959.96	128502.14
258	913.66	749.60	122411.52	306709.56	127588.48
259	918.99	744.27	123330.51	307453.83	126669.49
260	924.35	738.91	124254.86	308192.74	125745.14
261	929.75	733.51	125184.61	308926.25	124815.39
262	935.17	728.09	126119.78	309654.34	123880.22
263	940.63	722.63	127060.41	310376.97	122939.59
264	946.11	717.15	128006.52	311094.12	121993.48

265	951.63	711.63	128958.15	311805.75	121041.85
266	957.18	706.08	129915.33	312511.83	120084.67

267	962.77	700.49	130878.10	313212.32	119121.90
268	968.38	694.88	131846.48	313907.20	118153.52
269	974.03	689.23	132820.51	314596.43	117179.49
270	979.71	683.55	133800.22	315279.98	116199.78
271	985.43	677.83	134785.65	315957.81	115214.35
272	991.18	672.08	135776.83	316629.89	114223.17
273	996.96	666.30	136773.79	317296.19	113226.21
274	1002.77	660.49	137776.56	317956.68	112223.44
275	1008.62	654.64	138785.18	318611.32	111214.82
276	1014.51	648.75	139799.69	319260.07	110200.31

277	1020.42	642.84	140820.11	319902.91	109179.89
278	1026.38	636.88	141846.49	320539.79	108153.51
279	1032.36	630.90	142878.85	321170.69	107121.15
280	1038.39	624.87	143917.24	321795.56	106082.76
281	1044.44	618.82	144961.68	322414.38	105038.32
282	1050.54	612.72	146012.22	323027.10	103987.78
283	1056.66	606.60	147068.88	323633.70	102931.12
284	1062.83	600.43	148131.71	324234.13	101868.29
285	1069.03	594.23	149200.74	324828.36	100799.26
286	1075.26	588.00	150276.00	325416.36	99724.00
287	1081.54	581.72	151357.54	325998.08	98642.46
288	1087.85	575.41	152445.39	326573.49	97554.61

289	1094.19	569.07	153539.58	327142.56	96460.42
290	1100.57	562.69	154640.15	327705.25	95359.85
291	1106.99	556.27	155747.14	328261.52	94252.86
292	1113.45	549.81	156860.59	328811.33	93139.41
293	1119.95	543.31	157980.54	329354.64	92019.46
294	1126.48	536.78	159107.02	329891.42	90892.98
295	1133.05	530.21	160240.07	330421.63	89759.93
296	1139.66	523.60	161379.73	330945.23	88620.27

297	1146.31	516.95	162526.04	331462.18	87473.96
298	1153.00	510.26	163679.04	331972.44	86320.96
299	1159.72	503.54	164838.76	332475.98	85161.24
300	1166.49	496.77	166005.25	332972.75	83994.75

301	1173.29	489.97	167178.54	333462.72	82821.46
302	1180.13	483.13	168358.67	333945.85	81641.33
303	1187.02	476.24	169545.69	334422.09	80454.31
304	1193.94	469.32	170739.63	334891.41	79260.37
305	1200.91	462.35	171940.54	335353.76	78059.46
306	1207.91	455.35	173148.45	335809.11	76851.55
307	1214.96	448.30	174363.41	336257.41	75636.59
308	1222.05	441.21	175585.46	336698.62	74414.54
309	1229.18	434.08	176814.64	337132.70	73185.36
310	1236.35	426.91	178050.99	337559.61	71949.01
311	1243.56	419.70	179294.55	337979.31	70705.45
312	1250.81	412.45	180545.36	338391.76	69454.64

313	1258.11	405.15	181803.47	338796.91	68196.53
314	1265.45	397.81	183068.92	339194.72	66931.08
315	1272.83	390.43	184341.75	339585.15	65658.25
316	1280.25	383.01	185622.00	339968.16	64378.00
317	1287.72	375.54	186909.72	340343.70	63090.28
318	1295.23	368.03	188204.95	340711.73	61795.05
319	1302.79	360.47	189507.74	341072.20	60492.26
320	1310.39	352.87	190818.13	341425.07	59181.87
321	1318.03	345.23	192136.16	341770.30	57863.84
322	1325.72	337.54	193461.88	342107.84	56538.12
323	1333.45	329.81	194795.33	342437.65	55204.67
324	1341.23	322.03	196136.56	342759.68	53863.44

325	1349.06	314.20	197485.62	343073.88	52514.38
326	1356.93	306.33	198842.55	343380.21	51157.45

327	1364.84	298.42	200207.39	343678.63	49792.61
328	1372.80	290.46	201580.19	343969.09	48419.81
329	1380.81	282.45	202961.00	344251.54	47039.00
330	1388.87	274.39	204349.87	344525.93	45650.13
331	1396.97	266.29	205746.84	344792.22	44253.16
332	1405.12	258.14	207151.96	345050.36	42848.04
333	1413.31	249.95	208565.27	345300.31	41434.73
334	1421.56	241.70	209986.83	345542.01	40013.17
335	1429.85	233.41	211416.68	345775.42	38583.32
336	1438.19	225.07	212854.87	346000.49	37145.13

337	1446.58	216.68	214301.45	346217.17	35698.55
338	1455.02	208.24	215756.47	346425.41	34243.53
339	1463.51	199.75	217219.98	346625.16	32780.02
340	1472.04	191.22	218692.02	346816.38	31307.98
341	1480.63	182.63	220172.65	346999.01	29827.35
342	1489.27	173.99	221661.92	347173.00	28338.08
343	1497.95	165.31	223159.87	347338.31	26840.13
344	1506.69	156.57	224666.56	347494.88	25333.44
345	1515.48	147.78	226182.04	347642.66	23817.96
346	1524.32	138.94	227706.36	347781.60	22293.64
347	1533.21	130.05	229239.57	347911.65	20760.43
348	1542.16	121.10	230781.73	348032.75	19218.27

349	1551.15	112.11	232332.88	348144.86	17667.12
350	1560.20	103.06	233893.08	348247.92	16106.92
351	1569.30	93.96	235462.38	348341.88	14537.62
352	1578.46	84.80	237040.84	348426.68	12959.16
353	1587.66	75.60	238628.50	348502.28	11371.50
354	1596.93	66.33	240225.43	348568.61	9774.57
355	1606.24	57.02	241831.67	348625.63	8168.33
356	1615.61	47.65	243447.28	348673.28	6552.72
357	1625.04	38.22	245072.32	348711.50	4927.68

358	1634.52	28.74	246706.84	348740.24	3293.16
359	1644.05	19.21	248350.89	348759.45	1649.11
360	*1649.11	9.62	250000.00	348769.07	0.00

When you are young and trying to buy more house than you can afford, it can be costly. As an investor, you are expected to shop for rates and financing, and you are not supposed to get tied to a short-term loan that will cost you more than you could ever repay.

Bringing It All Together

As a real estate investor, you need to learn to finance your properties using all means of financing. Remember, your goals will be to find the best financing on the properties you buy taking into consideration factors such as loan terms, payment, and balloon options and much more.

Take a look at two examples below and you will see how the investor who proposed the deal saved more money by just asking for a lower interest rate and by kicking in some money up front. In example one, the seller offers to finance a $20,000 lot over five years with no money down at 10 percent interest. In example two, the buyer offers to pay $5,000 down for a lower interest rate of 5 percent. Take a look:

Example One will show a total amount of $25,496.40 repaid at the end with $5,496.40 paid in interest with a payment of $424.94.

Pmt	Principal	Interest	Cm Prin	Cm Int	Prin Bal
1	258.27	166.67	258.27	166.67	19741.73
2	260.43	164.51	518.70	331.18	19481.30
3	262.60	162.34	781.30	493.52	19218.70

4	264.78	160.16	1046.08	653.68	18953.92
5	266.99	157.95	1313.07	811.63	18686.93
6	269.22	155.72	1582.29	967.35	18417.71
7	271.46	153.48	1853.75	1120.83	18146.25
8	273.72	151.22	2127.47	1272.05	17872.53
9	276.00	148.94	2403.47	1420.99	17596.53
10	278.30	146.64	2681.77	1567.63	17318.23
11	280.62	144.32	2962.39	1711.95	17037.61
12	282.96	141.98	3245.35	1853.93	16754.65

13	285.32	139.62	3530.67	1993.55	16469.33
14	287.70	137.24	3818.37	2130.79	16181.63
15	290.09	134.85	4108.46	2265.64	15891.54
16	292.51	132.43	4400.97	2398.07	15599.03
17	294.95	129.99	4695.92	2528.06	15304.08
18	297.41	127.53	4993.33	2655.59	15006.67
19	299.88	125.06	5293.21	2780.65	14706.79
20	302.38	122.56	5595.59	2903.21	14404.41
21	304.90	120.04	5900.49	3023.25	14099.51
22	307.44	117.50	6207.93	3140.75	13792.07
23	310.01	114.93	6517.94	3255.68	13482.06
24	312.59	112.35	6830.53	3368.03	13169.47

25	315.19	109.75	7145.72	3477.78	12854.28
26	317.82	107.12	7463.54	3584.90	12536.46
27	320.47	104.47	7784.01	3689.37	12215.99
28	323.14	101.80	8107.15	3791.17	11892.85
29	325.83	99.11	8432.98	3890.28	11567.02
30	328.55	96.39	8761.53	3986.67	11238.47
31	331.29	93.65	9092.82	4080.32	10907.18
32	334.05	90.89	9426.87	4171.21	10573.13
33	336.83	88.11	9763.70	4259.32	10236.30
34	339.64	85.30	10103.34	4344.62	9896.66

35	342.47	82.47	10445.81	4427.09	9554.19
36	345.32	79.62	10791.13	4506.71	9208.87

37	348.20	76.74	11139.33	4583.45	8860.67
38	351.10	73.84	11490.43	4657.29	8509.57
39	354.03	70.91	11844.46	4728.20	8155.54
40	356.98	67.96	12201.44	4796.16	7798.56
41	359.95	64.99	12561.39	4861.15	7438.61
42	362.95	61.99	12924.34	4923.14	7075.66
43	365.98	58.96	13290.32	4982.10	6709.68
44	369.03	55.91	13659.35	5038.01	6340.65
45	372.10	52.84	14031.45	5090.85	5968.55
46	375.20	49.74	14406.65	5140.59	5593.35
47	378.33	46.61	14784.98	5187.20	5215.02
48	381.48	43.46	15166.46	5230.66	4833.54

49	384.66	40.28	15551.12	5270.94	4448.88
50	387.87	37.07	15938.99	5308.01	4061.01
51	391.10	33.84	16330.09	5341.85	3669.91
52	394.36	30.58	16724.45	5372.43	3275.55
53	397.64	27.30	17122.09	5399.73	2877.91
54	400.96	23.98	17523.05	5423.71	2476.95
55	404.30	20.64	17927.35	5444.35	2072.65
56	407.67	17.27	18335.02	5461.62	1664.98
57	411.07	13.87	18746.09	5475.49	1253.91
58	414.49	10.45	19160.58	5485.94	839.42
59	417.94	7.00	19578.52	5492.94	421.48
60	*421.48	3.51	20000.00	5496.45	-0.00

Example Two will show a total of $1,984.20 paid in interest, a lower monthly payment and a substantial savings of $3,512.20 realized all because the seller was willing to finance with a lower interest rate with a sizeable down payment.

Pmt	Principal	Interest	Cm Prin	Cm Int	Prin Bal
1	220.57	62.50	220.57	62.50	14779.43
2	221.49	61.58	442.06	124.08	14557.94
3	222.41	60.66	664.47	184.74	14335.53
4	223.34	59.73	887.81	244.47	14112.19
5	224.27	58.80	1112.08	303.27	13887.92
6	225.20	57.87	1337.28	361.14	13662.72
7	226.14	56.93	1563.42	418.07	13436.58
8	227.08	55.99	1790.50	474.06	13209.50
9	228.03	55.04	2018.53	529.10	12981.47
10	228.98	54.09	2247.51	583.19	12752.49
11	229.93	53.14	2477.44	636.33	12522.56
12	230.89	52.18	2708.33	688.51	12291.67

13	231.85	51.22	2940.18	739.73	12059.82
14	232.82	50.25	3173.00	789.98	11827.00
15	233.79	49.28	3406.79	839.26	11593.21
16	234.76	48.31	3641.55	887.57	11358.45
17	235.74	47.33	3877.29	934.90	11122.71
18	236.73	46.34	4114.02	981.24	10885.98
19	237.71	45.36	4351.73	1026.60	10648.27
20	238.70	44.37	4590.43	1070.97	10409.57
21	239.70	43.37	4830.13	1114.34	10169.87
22	240.70	42.37	5070.83	1156.71	9929.17
23	241.70	41.37	5312.53	1198.08	9687.47
24	242.71	40.36	5555.24	1238.44	9444.76

25	243.72	39.35	5798.96	1277.79	9201.04
26	244.73	38.34	6043.69	1316.13	8956.31
27	245.75	37.32	6289.44	1353.45	8710.56
28	246.78	36.29	6536.22	1389.74	8463.78
29	247.80	35.27	6784.02	1425.01	8215.98
30	248.84	34.23	7032.86	1459.24	7967.14

31	249.87	33.20	7282.73	1492.44	7717.27
32	250.91	32.16	7533.64	1524.60	7466.36
33	251.96	31.11	7785.60	1555.71	7214.40
34	253.01	30.06	8038.61	1585.77	6961.39
35	254.06	29.01	8292.67	1614.78	6707.33
36	255.12	27.95	8547.79	1642.73	6452.21

37	256.19	26.88	8803.98	1669.61	6196.02
38	257.25	25.82	9061.23	1695.43	5938.77
39	258.33	24.74	9319.56	1720.17	5680.44
40	259.40	23.67	9578.96	1743.84	5421.04
41	260.48	22.59	9839.44	1766.43	5160.56
42	261.57	21.50	10101.01	1787.93	4898.99
43	262.66	20.41	10363.67	1808.34	4636.33
44	263.75	19.32	10627.42	1827.66	4372.58
45	264.85	18.22	10892.27	1845.88	4107.73
46	265.95	17.12	11158.22	1863.00	3841.78
47	267.06	16.01	11425.28	1879.01	3574.72
48	268.18	14.89	11693.46	1893.90	3306.54

49	269.29	13.78	11962.75	1907.68	3037.25
50	270.41	12.66	12233.16	1920.34	2766.84
51	271.54	11.53	12504.70	1931.87	2495.30
52	272.67	10.40	12777.37	1942.27	2222.63
53	273.81	9.26	13051.18	1951.53	1948.82
54	274.95	8.12	13326.13	1959.65	1673.87
55	276.10	6.97	13602.23	1966.62	1397.77
56	277.25	5.82	13879.48	1972.44	1120.52
57	278.40	4.67	14157.88	1977.11	842.12
58	279.56	3.51	14437.44	1980.62	562.56
59	280.73	2.34	14718.17	1982.96	281.83
60	*281.83	1.17	15000.00	1984.13	0.00

As you finance your investments, remember nothing is ever set in stone and everything can be countered until the deal is final. Many investors believe no deal is ever final until it reaches the closing table. It is important to remember that in all aspects of a real estate transaction, everything is negotiable.

Chapter Thirteen

How to Promote Sales

This is the chapter you can use as your guide when you decide to offer your property for sale with creative financing options available. It will help you move your property when you are the seller in search of a buyer.

There will come a time when you need to be looking at financing creatively from the seller's viewpoint. You want to be able to offer other homeowners and investors the same opportunities you were given and be able to profit along the way.

Contrarians will go against what everyone else is doing. They will even remain in stalemate when the market appears to be booming, and they will be willing to sit tight while everyone else is wondering what to do next and racing to do something quickly. A contrarian is going to do the exact opposite in any investment situation. According to most, a contrarian appears to rebel against wisdom, against what is documented and sometimes even proven. However, the contrarian has the keen ability to make smart investments and also realize maximum profits over the long-term.

Why do you think contrarians succeed? They follow trends and are not afraid to use empirical research to make the best decisions possible for long-term investing and short-term speculation. They succeed because they will put forth the effort to research the historical data of past trends while looking to the future to provide more insight on what to expect in future markets. Contrarians are prepared and never influenced. They are ready with data and documents to analyze potential market turning points and are able to look at investment opportunities and see everything clearly.

Think about the mind-set of the macrowave investor whose perspective identifies sectors to invest in or to stay away from. They seem to know when to buy and when to sell before anyone else. They can see the future before anyone else, and it seems they never lose. Why are they always the leaders of the pack? Because they use data and analyze the markets that influence their investment, and they know three things:

- History repeats itself.

- What goes up will come down.

- What hits rock bottom has nowhere left to go but up.

Following trends and patterns in investing is advantageous to the macrowave investor. The macrowave investor knows if real estate in a particular area is at a record low, all is not lost. There is no hurry to dump the property because there will be a better time to sell later. They also realize when they are selling in a strong sellers' market that at any time it could shift. Pulling the property off the market can be advantageous to the seller during a buyers' market.

Throughout this book, you have discovered one of the key elements for being a successful speculator is patience. If you cannot exercise patience, you will lose money and if you are too eager to make money quickly or become greedy, you will quickly understand what it means to go for broke. Remember, being at the right place at the right time is everything, but leaving the scene too early or not sticking around for the best of times can be costly.

Selling When Everyone Is Selling

If you are going to sell in a buyers' market, the aggressive macrowave investor knows it is important to make your home or property as attractive as possible. Staging your home for a quick sale is important. Appealing to the masses is what you want to do if you are trying to stand out in a crowd.

An excellent resource for a seller looking to stage a home for a quicker sale is *301 Simple Things You Can Do to Sell Your Home NOW and For More Money Than You Thought: How to Reorganize, Stage, and Prepare Your Home for Sale* available from Atlantic Publishing (**www.atlantic-pub.com**, Item # 301-01).

The intelligent entrepreneur will try to avoid selling in a buyers' market but sometimes this is not possible. The best thing to do is to offer more options for the buyers who come along interested in buying.

The following are creative ideas for the macrowave investor selling at the wrong time:

- Offer to owner-finance the property to potential buyers.

You can carry a portion of the financing or the entire note depending on your current situation.

- Offer to rent-to-own the property. If you own the home free of liens and debts, this can be an ideal situation. You simply price the house and set an amount for the payments each month and ask an attorney to draw up the legal documents for you and the buyer. The tenant will become a homeowner with their final payment, and you can sell the home in a hot buyers' market using savvy business techniques to close the deal with a buyer who wants to buy but may have difficulty in obtaining the financing.

- Lease-purchase the home to someone with a portion of the lease applied toward the purchase.

- Lease-option the home to someone offering them the opportunity to lease until they exercise their option to buy or decline to exercise the option leaving you with their deposit and the monthly income you gained by someone occupying the property.

- Offer to rent the property straight out rather than selling when it is a buyers' market which is making it impossible for you to get a fair price for your real estate.

After you are familiar with the macrowave investing concepts and money is not a big concern for you in your investments, you should be able to sell at the appropriate times and buy when it is most advantageous for you to buy.

What Really Affects the Time to Sell

The Federal Reserve is one of the biggest factors in real estate. Everyone knows that when the Fed meets and interest rates go up, the real estate market temporarily goes flat. Then as if it never happened, homes begin to move again and sellers place their homes on the market.

While the Fed can certainly kick a dent in the home seller's front door, there are other factors that warrant your attention, too, which the contrarian will use to make decisions investment decisions. Contrary to what everyone else believes, they will prove the market to be profitable based on their decisions.

A flat market means it is just wise to wait before selling. For instance, if you are the owner of an oceanfront condo in the middle of the strip in Virginia Beach, Virginia, placing the condo on the market at the end of September is not the best move for you because the season is over. Winters there can be too chilly for beachfront living. With the streets quiet and the town empty, a would-be investor who might be interested in buying the condo would probably want it at a discount.

Holding on to investments in real estate can often prove difficult especially if you have many property holdings in a particular area that appear to be thriving one minute and then at the bitter end the next. This is why it is so important to use various means of financing and never have all your real estate holdings in one area of the market at any time especially when you are just starting out with your investments.

If you are diversifying, you should be able to find market conditions prime at any given time. You should be able to find areas that are great for buyers and other areas prime for selling.

As an investor of real estate, keep your options open to a variety of real estate investments. The macrowave investor will go into one area and see opportunity to build a condominium complex for retirees because baby boomers are approaching retirement. In another area, he or she may go into the market realizing the need for more student housing near a college campus. While he is developing two separate housing complexes in two separate areas, right in his backyard, he finds property is not moving. No one is buying and no one is selling, so he sits still and when he tires of sitting on the property, he rents it or he offers to owner-finance it to someone else.

An investor of real estate keeps the following in mind:

- Where the market is today

- Where it was yesterday

- Where will it go tomorrow

The reason a macrowave investor will always come out on top is because of his ability to analyze the market in anything he or she does. Collect and analyze data. Take the time to know your investment business.

Where the Market is Today

Find out what the market is doing today. If it helps you to keep notes or a journal, take the time to collect data and store them on your computer. Take the time to watch CNBC and listen to commentary on the housing sector. Subscribe to online newsletters and join investment groups online such as the Yahoo!

Groups and other business-related forums. If you take a look at past trends and cycles, you should be able to foresee where the real estate market is headed. It is important to learn to analyze data, gather research, and use all the tools you have at your disposal so you can make smart investment choices tomorrow.

Ask Questions

While questioning everything can be good, macrowave investors know if they become consumed with questioning every element within the market, they will waste time. The investor who asks too many questions will miss opportunities and be easily drawn into situations they should avoid.

Today there are more homeowners and more foreclosures than ever before.

How to Finance Your Real Estate (to Buyers Who Want to Buy)

As a seller, the first thing you should consider doing after you decide to sell is to list the property for sale with creative financing available. Decide which approach you want to take. Do you want to offer your properties as a rent-to-own or as owner-financed? One difference in the two is the timing for you to transfer the title of ownership. However, in a rent-to-own property, there can potentially be more hassles for the seller down the road.

Many investors prefer owner-financing because the sale goes through the closing process with all the closing perks. For instance, in a real estate transaction with seller-financing, the real estate agents involved or the seller and buyer will line up things such as an appraisal, home inspection, and title search before closing on the property. In a rent-to-own, this does not happen. In some seller-financing deals, a buyer will not ask for an appraisal or survey but they should care enough about their investment to ask for a title search and a home inspection. If a real estate agent is involved, he or she will handle all these details for the seller who is providing a purchase-money mortgage and everything will be taken care of just as it would in a traditional lender's closing.

If you choose to go the route of seller-financing, you need to make it clear that you will foreclose if the buyer defaults. When you go from real estate investor to seller-offering-financing, your new role as the lender will force you to play hard ball when it comes to protecting your interests. As a landlord, you will be forced to serve eviction notices and often ask your tenants to move and that alone is tough. However, when you are the lender and hold a purchase-money mortgage on a piece of property, it is another ball game altogether when you begin to foreclose on someone's home.

Finding the Best Approach

If you are uncomfortable with your potential buyers for any reason, it may be best to find another buyer because financing a property to someone is a lasting relationship in many cases. If you think your buyers cannot afford the home or property you are selling, you may want to have an attorney draw up an air tight and binding contract with in a rent-to-own transaction. If you move forward with buyers you are uneasy about, take a moment to consider rent-to-own versus owner-financing to your clients because a rent-to-own scenario is easier to deal with in case an eviction is necessary. Foreclosures are headaches and in some cases, they can be expensive.

The Best Buyer a Seller Can Have

The best buyer a seller can hope to have is one who first approaches you as the seller with a plan of action. As a seller, you want to have a buyer who shows you they cannot only afford your home but they can also show you how they can and will pay you.

Take a look at the various amortization tables in the appendix and you will quickly understand how easy it is to be a seller who can make a fortune by owner-financing. In fact, if you are an investor who can afford to carry the paper on the properties you sell. This is the best way to make money on your real estate transactions. If you are going to flip properties, try to carry as much of the paper as you possibly can.

The best buyers a seller can have are those who have their own financing in order minus their down payment and closing costs. A seller, who recognizes the fact that he or she can help a buyer find a way to purchase the real estate he wants to purchase, can enable a buyer to buy and garner interest on the money the buyer needs to borrow.

As a seller, if you are listening to the goals of a buyer whenever you make the decision to sell on a purchase-money mortgage or using creative financing, you should be able to find a way to realize your dreams while the buyer realizes his or her dreams, too.

Real estate investors know the advantages of using a real estate agent when they are buying and after you begin selling creatively, you will see the advantages in using a real estate agent to sell your property creatively. In fact, you will probably never want to dabble in real estate without an agent only because they can save you time. When you list your property for sale with an agent, be sure to explain you are planning to sell the property using creative financing. Discuss the options you will consider. The following are some of the options you may have:

- Rent-to-own

- Seller-financing on a purchase-money mortgage

- Lease Option

- Assumable Mortgage

Do not mislead your buyers into thinking you have an assumable mortgage anyone can assume. In most cases, an assumable loan can only be assumed by someone deemed credit-worthy by the lender who financed you. There are often several options for you to consider when you are acting as the banker. Find the one where you profit most with as little aggravation as possible.

Chapter Fourteen

On the Contrary, I Am Speculating Successfully

L earning to be a contrarian investor can certainly put you at the forefront of the markets where you invest but only if you know what you are doing. The contrarian mindset pays off when you are using it to obtain properties which are obtainable using creative measures to secure your loans. It pays off when you have the cash to use to your advantage when everyone else is interested in selling. It pays off when you do things differently than everyone else and it proves to lead you to more profits.

Part of acting on investments is knowing what you want to gain through your investments. Do you want an investment to pay you a monthly income through tenant renting? Are you handy with a saw and paint brush so that you prefer the handy-man specials? Do you prefer the commercial leasing end of the real estate sector, or are you driven to develop large subdivisions?

In addition to knowing where you want to stake your claim, you also need to decide where is your interest? And wherever your interests lie, that is where you should be in your real estate endeavors.

Before you spend your first dime in the real estate market, you need to read, research, and study. Know the market by studying what outside factors can cause a shift in the market where you are investing. Talk to other investors about how they are investing and learn from older and wiser investors who are willing to talk to you.

Investors who are in the game of real estate are not eager to share their knowledge of buying and selling real estate with other would-be investors because of competition. Investors do not need competition driving up the cost of handy-man specials and vacant lots. They do not want to get into a bidding war with new investors at foreclosure auctions. In a nutshell, they would like to keep competition to a minimum to keep prices affordable. Of course, the more affordable a property is, the more profits the investor can realize.

Investors who deal in real estate look for the most inexpensive way to do it. Some of them will take lavish measures to find creative ways to finance their investments. They will look for ways to finance their homes and property and they will find the best way to work out a deal when conditions indicate a strong buyers' market.

These same investors will sell in a strong sellers' market when they had no plans of doing so, and they will take the initiative to connect with a buyer when it is most advantageous to sell and walk away with a profit they can be proud to make. When the market is flushing out the potential for sales, they talk to their agent about moving forward by offering to finance their properties to buyers creatively. As investors, they hold no personal attachments to any property they own and will sell it when the market indicates it is best to flip it and move on to something else. Real estate investors are in control of their money and their investments. They even are in control of the market to some extent.

Property collectors have different investing styles. They each have certain strategies they use in their investing techniques and their own way of doing things. Investors have preferences in many areas of real estate. Some investors prefer to buy handyman specials while others prefer to stick to commercial investing with leasing space as their primary objective. Still, investors who are conscious of what the market is doing will change the way they do business if it is more profitable to them. If they can make more money one way over another, they quickly change their strategy to accommodate market trends so they too can cash in on market changes.

The Contrarian Collects Real Estate, Not Dust

A contrarian in the stock market will buy stocks he knows no one else wants or he will sell when everyone else is buying. He goes against what he is told and what everyone else is doing. The contrarian does not just run out and try to do the opposite of other investors, but he finds a reason to go against what everyone else is doing and in many cases, it pays off fabulously.

The long-term investor of real estate follows trends and using market news and crucial research successfully invests in the appropriate areas of the market by being a contrarian. Real estate contrarians know that even when the economy is good, real estate can be volatile but they also know the volatility in the real estate market is never as uncertain as the stock market. As players in the housing market, they are never easily scared by outside factors. For example, when everyone is scared off by any news of an interest rate hike, an investor will quickly unload a property on a buyer and finance it at the prime rate or he will purchase a new property from a seller who is scared by the latest news on rising interest rates, snapping up a property with seller-financing at a lower adjustable rate or prime rate.

A contrarian who goes against the norm can become one of the more savvy real estate investors because he will go against what everyone else is doing, and most of the time he can accumulate properties much faster because he does not depend on loan approvals from traditional lenders. A book called *52 Homes in 52 Weeks* written by Dolf De Roos, Ph.D., and Gene Burns lays the groundwork for acquiring properties quickly. A contrarian who adopts the mind-set of financing without the help of traditional lenders *and* adopts the concepts used in *52 Homes in 52 Weeks* can pad their investment portfolio quickly.

If you are investing in real estate, it is important to know when to buy and sell and how to finance the real estate you purchase. Even wealthy real estate investors choose to finance their property purchases using the best strategies for creative financing simply because in certain markets, a traditional home mortgage loan just is not always the smartest way to finance. In the following pages we are going to discuss some of the best ways to finance creatively.

Speculating Successfully Using Purchase-Money Mortgages

A purchase-money mortgage occurs when a seller chooses to provide financing for a property he or she owns. As an investor, you may feel this is a bad idea but look at how it can be advantageous for the seller to finance a credit-worthy buyer's purchase, and how it is often more attractive for the buyer or investor to work with a seller.

In a purchase-money mortgage, a seller will provide financing to the buyer instead of a buyer's going to a bank. As an investor, there are several reasons to approach a seller to handle your financing even if you have excellent credit. Following are several reasons for the investor to consider approaching the seller for creative financing.

- The seller may be able to offer a better interest rate.

- Often the overall closing costs can be discounted when dealing with a seller providing a purchase-money mortgage rather than with a bank or mortgage company.

- The investor may want to finance the property through a seller and work out terms such as a monthly mortgage payment of a certain amount while paying a balloon payment each year. Investors can work out quarterly payments and delayed payments with a willing seller more easily than with a traditional lender.

- Depending on how the deal is worked out on paper, the buyer can keep his debt-to-income ratio down because the seller will not be reporting the debt to the credit bureaus.

This is an advantage for the buyer because he keeps his credit free to buy other properties that might require a lower debt-ratio.

The problem investors have in seller-financing is finding properties where the seller is capable of carrying the paper on the property. Most of the time, even if sellers are willing to carry financing for a property, they cannot carry it to the point of becoming a wealthy real estate investor. In other words, they may be able to carry it for a certain period of time but in some cases, an investor would be better off to go through a bank if the seller is unable to be extremely flexible on terms. Remember, as an investor, your main goal is to make deals where it is advantageous to you, and this means using financial terms that are most advantageous to yourself.

When people think of seller-financing, they think of a purchase-money mortgage being provided by a seller because the buyer cannot afford to pay for the property. Nothing is further from the truth for the seller who provides financing to the savvy investor. Depending on trends within the market, interest rates, and other factors, it is just smart business for an investor to find a way to use seller-financing and a purchase-money mortgage.

Assumable Mortgages

In Chapter 10, we looked at assumable loans. Most people think about the FHA and VA loans when they hear the term "assumable loan," a term that brings to mind first-time homeowners and people with poor credit. Yet, the assumable mortgage allows investors to assume an existing mortgage and often makes buying an investment more attractive for the following reasons:

- An assumable mortgage usually makes it to the closing table quicker than a new loan.

- Terms are far more attractive with an assumable loan than with a new loan.

- Buyers with a higher debt-to-income ratio—which is typical of the average new investor—can assume a loan much easier than obtaining a new one.

- Speculators like the convenience of the assumable loans and having terms that bind a seller to the assumable.

As an investor who is using an assumable loan, you should check out other loans before you just accept the terms and conditions of the current assumable loan on the property. The assumable loan may have a higher interest rate than the investor can secure, and it may also carry terms and conditions the investor, as a buyer, will not find acceptable. However, the assumable makes it easy for the investor who is pushing the limit with his debt-to-income ratio to get into a property with less money. However, it is best to check out all your options for financing, particularly if you have excellent credit and collateral.

Second Mortgages and Investing

Second mortgages can be helpful in financing an investor's properties. From the buyer's standpoint, a second mortgage can be taken out on an existing property to help secure financing of future properties. Second mortgages can be used effectively by real estate investors when they are working with investment properties and need the seller to provide assistance in financing. They are used by smart investors who are trying to buy more property while market conditions are prime for investors but banks are unwilling to carry all the risk.

Often, these mortgages enable a speculator to secure funds quickly for a seller who needs to sell in a hurry. If time is of the essence, often a seller will sell to the buyer who can close the quickest while buyers are in a bidding war for the property. The investor who can secure funds quickly and race to the closing table is much more appealing to the seller who needs to sell and move on quickly to another location or deal.

Using Options to Speculate in Real Estate

Smart contrarians are option-prone when it comes to speculating because they can do what they do best—go against the norm and profit handsomely. In Chapter 7, we discussed why options are smart to use in real estate transactions. The investor who learns how to maneuver options will enjoying using them in real estate investments, and the contrarian will find them lucrative when speculating in real property because options give the risky contrarian a way to test the waters: options are safe for this investor. They allow the investor to buy real estate, in a sense, with little money and little risk if the investor exercises care in choosing options.

An option is something an investor purchases to give himself the ability to buy or sell his interest in a property during a designated time. After an investor secures a legal option on a piece of property, he is able to control what the true, original owner does with it. More important, the investor can take out an option and sell it before they actually buy the property or pay for it.

Here are several reasons to use an option to buy real estate.

- Options are often used to secure a property while a buyer puts together a creative financing package.

- The most advantageous way for a buyer or investor to use options is for the buyer to secure an option to buy for a set amount and a length of six months for example. During that time, the buyer will try to secure another buyer for the property at a higher sales price. At closing, the investor makes a profit and moves on to another property. It is a great way to secure a deal for the seller while giving the investor an opportunity to make quick money on an option to buy.

- An option is used to tie up a property that a buyer really wants but cannot afford.

- A contrarian uses options to gain leverage in the real estate market allowing himself to buy when everyone else is selling and then sell when everyone else is buying.

Using options can be risky in certain markets. An investor who goes into a buyers' market and offers to take an option for a set amount with unrealistic time conditions can make a costly investment with dubious results. On the flip side, if a smart capitalist begins to accumulate options when no one is buying and manages his time constraints well, he can make a fortune by making sure the options are exercised when everyone begins to buy again. This allows him to profit when he sells the properties covered with options.

Private Investors and the Contrarian

In any market, you can use the services of a private investor to finance your home or real estate purchases. However, you should realize an investor may want different terms than you want with due consideration to current market conditions. At this point your credit will be a strong factor in whether you are able to get the financing you need through a private investor.

Contrarians are accused of using private investors simply because doing so is contrary to usual procedure. A private investor will hold the property as collateral using a purchase-money mortgage or may be willing to go into an arrangement with the buyer where the investor is considered part-owner of the property through a shared-equity agreement. The private investor is considered risky as a business partner, but there can be some positive results from the relationship.

In some cases, the shared-equity can be a bad financial move for the buyer of the property. Investors who are speculating in real estate may use the services of an outside investor initially, but after they have accumulated several properties, they have no need for another investor. There are some special circumstances where it may be unavoidable. However, the private investor is not considered the most desirable way to finance your investments as an investor.

Private investors can help a new investor get started in real estate and teach the new investor about the market, but they can be the death of your profit, too. Investing with a private investor means they will not cut you some slack if you are a new investor with good credit. Therefore, you are better off going to a bank or through your seller if you want to secure creative financing.

However, the private investor still appeals to the contrarian because of the flexibility and the lowered risk, in some cases, which a private investor may offer another investor.

The Property Collector's Portfolio

A true collector of property may have much capital to work with one year and few dollars in his account the next. He or she will see their cash flow change significantly because of too much turnover in tenant-dominated properties. This is where it is advantageous for the investor to know as much as possible about market conditions and how the outside world can affect the real estate market. Smart investors of real estate watch the following for indicators on the real estate market.

- They watch interest rates.

- They watch the local area market where they buy and sell real estate.

- They look at market trends throughout the world.

- They follow past indicators.

In a nutshell, they collect data. Then they do the opposite of what everyone else is doing. An investor who dabbles in real estate and the stock market feels comfortable with his or her investments in real estate for two main reasons:

- Even when the market falls in real estate, it recovers quickly and seldom is viewed as a mainstay among investors. Time heals all battle wounds for the real estate investor.

- The stock market has suffered crashes or detrimental set-backs within one business day of trading. Real estate declines slowly when it begins to tank. It is not something that happens overnight. Could property values drop dramatically overnight? It is possible but not likely unless there is a major natural disaster such the catastrophe of Hurricane Katrina.

A property collector has historical data on his or her side when considering the safety net of the real estate market, and the trader — specifically the day trader — has historical proof that nothing in life is guaranteed. The property collector realizes it is possible to lose money on a property but highly unlikely if he or she is able to hang on to it and ride out declining markets.

As an investor in real estate, learn to buy what the masses are not buying. Train yourself to be a contrarian but do not buy something because you realize no one else is buying. Study the market and the trends and try to predict future demand.

In real estate, a contrarian will purchase handy-man specials in a run-down area. He will go in and buy several in a specific area, fix up the homes, and when he has several ready, he will sell them, or he may rent them until market conditions are ripe to sell.

The neat thing about the contrarian in real estate is that as a real estate investor, he or she can change the real estate market in particular areas. Look at Donald Trump and consider some of the projects he has taken on as a real estate investor. Some of the areas where he started his fortune were considered risky investments at the time, but he went in and built an empire taking risks and going against the masses. Donald Trump is one of the most successful contrarians in the business of real estate. He has proven going against the masses can make real estate investors extremely wealthy.

As an investor of real estate, remember you want to buy in different areas going against the trend of the masses, and you also want to diversify. There are some areas where it is wise to be a landlord and accumulate properties that allow you to do so with a good cash flow. There are some areas where land is cheap and it would be advisable to buy it up at a reasonable price to build on later. There are other markets where you may find lakefront property at an all-time low or a devastated area where a natural disaster has made it possible to pick up some handy-man specials. In other words, as an investor, you are not limited to purchasing only homes, rental units, or apartment complexes. The savvy investor knows the market is wide open, and the intelligent investor buys different types of properties in various markets.

Other Thoughts on Your Real Property Collection

Before you begin "collecting" real estate, you should probably consider how much working capital you have for things like repairs and updates as well as general upkeep until you either resell the property or rent it. I highly recommend that you develop a checklist to use as a guideline when you are in the market for investments.

Your checklist would include the following.

- People want to be in a convenient location. Even if wide-open spaces are important, the ability to get to the mall or grocery store in a few minutes can be equally important. Convenience should be considered for every investment you make. Even contrarians will watch the location factor because so many individuals were raised on the theory of location…location…location.

- Choose investment properties near you. If you are developing a subdivision a couple of hours from your home, you will not be available to the crews who may need you. If you are not near the areas where you invest, make arrangements to rent an apartment nearby or hire a manager or foreman.

- Go where the masses will not go but do not go where they will never go. Not everyone can gamble on the West Side and win. You have to know your market and the general area and where the shift is going to be. For instance in Nashville, Tennessee, growth is evident everywhere, but the savvy investor who can think years ahead will see Columbia as the better place to develop because the shift is in that direction. Columbia does not offer cultural events but being only 30 minutes from Nashville, it offers the best in open spaces near a big city. Author Peter Navarro speaks about the macrowave investor who will see towns like Columbia as a gold mine waiting to be discovered.

- Learn from the advice of others in the industry but never get in the habit of following it. Remember you are an investor who goes against what the masses are doing and often the advice you receive weighs heavily on what others are currently doing in the market. The contrarian needs to know what others are doing but only to ensure he is not doing the same thing.

- Never pay full price unless you are sure it is a fair market price. This is why a real estate broker can help you in the industry. For instance, if you find an apartment building at a modest $200,000 in the city, and you are certain it is a good deal, have a real estate agent look up some comparable properties for you and help you with a market analysis. See if the apartment building serves your long-term and short-term investment needs and, thinking ahead, decide if it serves your intended purpose as an investment.

- No matter how you are going to pay for or finance the investments you buy, you have to be sure you can afford what you buy. Can you make the payments each month even when a tenant-occupied property is vacant? Can *you* afford the property you are buying? Do you like the way the terms are for the property you are buying? If not, find another way to finance the property which will appeal to you most.

- Even in seller-financed properties, as a smart investor you should have the appraisal complete on the property before you close the sale. An appraisal is crucial when you are borrowing money from a traditional lender, and it can give you peace of mind in deals where the seller is carrying the purchase-money mortgage.

- Expect fair dealings and deliver fair dealings. Often, if you are lucky in real estate, outsiders will view you as shrewd. Remember in the world of investing, it is much better to be considered shrewd than broke. Be shrewd in your business dealings but always be fair and expect the same in all your business transactions.

A business investor who is keen on buying and selling real estate for profit must demand fair, honest dealings because the more property he or she accumulates the more important they will become. As an investor, you want to know everything you can about the investments you represent, and you will not be able to deliver good housing if you are not certain of what you have bought. Insist on home inspections, appraisals, termite inspections, and full disclosures on the properties. If you ever deal with a real estate broker who does not deliver on the things you expect, do not use him or her again.

Overpriced and Climbing

People refer to stocks as *undervalued* or to the stock market as being *bullish* or *bearish.* In real estate, investors use the terms *sellers' ma*rket and *buyers' market.* How they react in each market can affect their bottom line at the end of the year, just as it will if they were working against the market and a margin call pulls them back into reality.

Expensive, overpriced stocks can always unnerve the analyst who likes to keep things simple. Yet even when analysts advise to short a stock, there are those who choose to keep buying a stock convinced it is ready to hit another 52-week high. In real estate, overpriced properties can easily be disguised in many different facets. For instance, when a seller is more than willing to finance a property creatively, insisting on a rapid closing, red warning flags should start waving in your mind.

As an investor, you are at risk for the eager-to-carry-the-paper seller with ulterior motives. For instance, when an investor approaches a seller for creative financing, most of the time they still expect that seller to sell their property at a fair market price. Using comparative market analysis, a buyer should know what the property is worth or they can find out the information quickly by looking it up at the courthouse. Still, a seller can sell at any price they want and often, they find a way to sell at a higher price when they finance the property carrying a purchase-money mortgage.

A seller who raises a price on the buyer because he or she is financing the property is making a fortune because in addition to hiking the price, the seller is collecting interest. Not only did the price of real estate just go up but it is rapidly climbing, at least from the buyer's standpoint. When this happens, the buyer should run. Why? For example, you have an 1,800 square foot home you are purchasing from a seller who is carrying the paper on the residence. He is offering a purchase-money mortgage and the fair price for the home is $240,000. At the end of 10 years, collecting 6.5 percent interest, the seller will make an additional $87,018.28 on $240,000 — not to mention that with a credit-worthy buyer, the seller can look forward to consistent monthly payments of $2,725.15. Not a bad income for a seller. Furthermore, if the housing market is bad and homes are not moving, the seller who would not be able to sell any other way can quickly move the property and realize a greater profit by simply providing the buyer with a purchase-money mortgage.

Many areas are overpriced even without the help of a seller making a mint from a property he is willing to finance — because he knows the property will never appraise for enough money to secure a loan from a bank. For instance, in June 2006 *Forbes* magazine released some photos of the most expensive homes in the United States. For a cool $20 million, a 40-acre estate could be yours in Carmel, Indiana. If you think $20 million is a bit much for a 40-acre estate in Indiana, maybe you will find $125 million more reasonable along the coast, more specifically in Palm Beach, Florida. Right down the road from that gorgeous home, $45 million pays for 24,000 square feet of living space but it has a waterfront too so what more can you ask for?

Hulk Hogan's posh estate was recently available in Bellair, Florida, for only $25 million, and in Naples for around the same price investors could own the pinkest house on the market. An older home in Malibu costs $65 million, but it does sit pretty as you please in the middle of six acres. Overpriced? You better believe it. For $46.5 million, a home in lovely Hawaii on the sea could be yours, including barn, stable, and corral. Overpriced? In comparison to the other multi-million dollar mansions, not at all. In fact, this one was the best of the lot, but perhaps the Palm Beach home at $125 million had a better location or more precisely, a more prestigious address.

Overpriced estates owned by the rich and famous are beyond reach of the average person's income, but because these estate owners are able to demand prices that are out of this world, they help the market for high-end homes. If Hulk Hogan can get $25 million, should his neighbor be able to command the same price? Even in the higher-end markets, the ripple effect is evident in pricing, investing, and trends. These homes are just an indication of where the real estate market is headed.

The contrarian investor is able to capitalize in areas where the market appears to have great potential with prices growing faster than the average found anywhere else. Overpriced properties tend to cluster together. For instance, in Malibu many of the older homes are on the market at incredibly high prices but if the same home were in the mountains of Colorado, it would be valued at one-quarter the asking price in Malibu.

Investors who are willing to buy overpriced properties take a risk that the market will improve to support the higher end homes. Still, according to many analysts who watch the housing sector, there will come a time when the overpriced homes of the world will need to show promise with gifted updates and substantial remodeling before a buyer will be interested. If this is true, homes owned by the affluent would eventually be considered risk-ridden investments with the potential for substantial loss when returning to the market.

Shoulda, Coulda, Woulda

Everyone has heard the heart-felt sentiments of would-be investors. "I should have known it was the right time to buy" or "I could have made better investment decisions" or "We would have bought if we had known it was going to be such a good investment" and so on. A long time ago, I was told, "Shoulda never coulda because they never woulda." I had no idea what it meant until I was older. If you "should have" (for instance, bought real estate) but you never "could" (buy or invest), it was because you never "would."

Real estate investors are not afraid to diversify in their real estate holdings and they know the more they hold in real property, the better their bottom line looks at the end of the year. That is, of course, assuming the real estate investor knows what he or she is doing and makes the right business moves. The investor who can plan effectively what he will do with every property he buys can profit most from the investments he makes.

The smart real estate investor knows he cannot just throw in the towel after making investments. Instead, he knows he must continue to make the right choices for the properties he holds.

Like the millionaire CEO who struggles to make it to the top of the corporate ladder, After he gets there, he works as hard as ever before to maintain his position and affluent lifestyle. He wants to stay there.

In real estate, after you have started accumulating properties, you want to hold on to them. You want to be able to use them to generate profit and you want to purchase more because it becomes a chess match of sorts. After you own properties you want to continue investing in real estate; therefore, it is important to know what to do with them as you are accumulating real estate for your portfolio.

Even though it sounds like a tedious undertaking to sink your money into the real estate sector, the fact is, everyone *should* invest. Everyone *can* invest but those who do not, do not because they just *will not*. For whatever reason, they choose to avoid investments. They choose to settle for their life as they know it because it is comfortable and safe. It feels better to let someone else take all the risks and then sit back and wish you had done something a bit differently. However, I promise you one thing, if you sit back and wait, you will not profit. You will not become the kind of investor you want to become because you are not an investor if you are not speculating.

In real estate, there are doers and there are dreamers. Which are you?

Conclusion

I hope you have enjoyed *How to Creatively Finance Your Real Estate Investments and Build Your Personal Fortune: What Smart Investors Need to Know — Explained Simply.* It was written to help you see the money trail and possibly the money.

Real estate is not a get-rich-quick scheme. It is a viable tool to use to accumulate massive wealth, and it is a tool that will be around for as long as you are around to use it. Is it a way to get rich quick? Oh yes, absolutely. It is not a hustle. If it is, then talk to the old money families who have been accumulating wealth for a long time and ask them how they feel about it.

Extraordinary lives are being built using the wealth accumulated through real estate. You see, real estate offers to open more doors for you than any other means today. You can invest in real estate no matter where you are, and if you are an investor who is interested in pursuing real estate as a full-time career, you can work from anywhere in the world.

I missed opportunities to accumulate real estate while I was in the business and the opportunities I took turned out to be bad investments so if I sound like a know-it-all, I am here to tell you, I learned my lessons the hard way. Now, thanks to research (and writing), I am finally able to share in some of the better ones. Remember, as you begin to invest in the properties you like, find the financing that makes you most comfortable and learn from everyone you meet so that you can make the most of every opportunity.

Here is the reason I like the lease-options best. In real estate, my husband and I bought a condo in the city when we were first married and we intended to stay there for some time. Luckily, we bought the condo on a lease-option contract. Sure, we lost our deposit and the money set aside to be used toward the purchase of the condo because we decided to get out of the deal. However, if we had bought the condo straight out, it would have made a miserable investment. Because it was so easy to get out of the deal, I have been fond of leases ever since. If you ever want to begin accumulating property without everyone knowing your business and you can keep a handle on what you are doing so you are certain not to over-extend yourself — lease-options are the way to go.

As we close, I want to thank you for buying this book and now, I encourage you to get out there and buy something that will help you build a solid future for you and those you love — real estate!

Glossary of Terms

A

ABSTRACT OF TITLE A matter of public record, a title company or someone in the attorney's office will take the initiative to view this to be sure a clean title, or deed, to the property is available when the property is sold and before it is closed.

ACCEPTANCE A term used when the buyer's offer to purchase is approved by the seller.

ACCOUNTANT The person responsible for helping the agent file their taxes and keep up with their tax obligations.

ACRE 43,560 square feet.

ADJUSTABLE RATE MORTGAGE (ARM) A mortgage that is subject to change based on interest rates, and the payment varies.

AFTER REPAIR VALUE (ARV) Used to determine a property's true value after repairs have been taken care of on the property in question.

AGENT A person who represents another person. In real estate, the agent represents the seller or the buyer.

AGREEMENT OF SALE An agreement between buyer and seller where both parties agree to the terms of the written contract for the real estate transaction.

AMORTIZATION Used in financial transactions where loans are calculated using installments.

APARTMENT ASSOCIATION A group of apartment owners who meet at a scheduled time to determine the needs of the property in question and decide on general maintenance issues.

APPRAISAL A formal, written estimate that details the value of real estate.

APPRAISER A person who is licensed to prepare appraisals for real estate transactions. FHA uses an FHA-approved list.

APPRECIATION The financial growth in a property's value as appraised worth over a period of time.

ASSIGNMENT This is a document which a buyer can use to assign the terms of their contract to someone else.

ASSUMPTION OF MORTGAGE A clause used in mortgage documents permitting a new buyer to take over the mortgage in question.

B

BALLOON PAYMENT This is a payment due at the end of the term of a particular mortgage. Most of the time a mortgage payment will be made for a specific number of months and the balance will balloon and become due in full at the end of the pre-determined term. This is used in many owner-financing deals where the owner will finance a property for a buyer who pays interest only until the end of a specific time. Then the buyer obtains his own mortgage through a traditional lender, and the balloon payment will be satisfied with the original seller.

BENEFICIARY The person who receives benefits from an estate through execution of a will or document.

BINDER A good-faith monetary retainer to hold the property and show the intent to buy it.

BIRD DOG A person who tries to locate properties for an individual investor in exchange for a fee.

BLANKET MORTGAGE Mortgage covering two pieces of property to secure a note. Often called an overlapping mortgage.

BRIDGE LOAN A loan adjoining two loans together. Commonly used to join the new purchase loan and a previous loan into one loan with both properties. Used to help a buyer close on his present home purchase before his other home sells.

BROKER A person who brings buyer and seller together in real estate transactions for a fee or commission.

C

CAPITAL GAINS Any profit made on a property when it is sold minus any home improvements and the original cost of the real estate in question.

CASH FLOW Difference between starting money or cash on hand and ending money on hand.

CAVEAT EMPTOR "Let the buyer beware." Sometimes used in a legal document to encourage buyers to take precautions when buying the property.

CHAIN OF TITLE Tells the story of the title or deed. Explains who owned the property and anything significant about the title of a property.

CLEAR TITLE A deed to a property free of liens.

CLOUD ON THE TITLE Something that stands out on a title that can cause a transaction to fall through because the lender or the buyer finds suspicion in the defect on the title.

CLOSING A meeting where the seller legally transfers real estate to the buyer.

CLOSING COSTS The buyer's and seller's closing fees, which they need to satisfy at the closing of the real estate transfer.

CLOSING STATEMENT A document that lists all fees associated with the real estate transaction at hand. Most people will receive it before closing.

COLLATERAL Something attached to secure financing. For example, in home mortgages, the home is put up for collateral for the money borrowed for the purchase.

COMMERCIAL PROPERTY A term used to describe business property not intended for residential purposes.

COMMISSION A fee based on a percent of the selling price of the property.

COMPARABLE MARKET ANALYSIS Used to compare properties in the same area to determine property value. Agents use this tool to determine a fair market price for real estate.

CONDITIONAL SALES CONTRACT Often considered the same as a contingency contract. This is a sales contract that is only enforced if conditions are satisfied.

CONTRACT A legal document which is enforceable under law if written appropriately and signed by all parties involved.

COSIGNER A person other than the primary signer of a loan or note indicating that the cosigner agrees to take over financial obligations if the original signer cannot.

D

DEED Proof in writing that the real estate belongs to the person in question; it is the same as title to the property.

DEED OF TRUST A deed recorded which indicates protection to the mortgage holder by guaranteeing the lender position as the lender for the financial means to acquire the property.

DEFAULT Not making a payment on a debt means being in default on the loan.

DEPRECIATION Property decreasing in value is shown

to depreciate or to show depreciation.

DISCOUNTED PROPERTIES Properties priced below appraised value.

DOWN PAYMENT The amount of money the buyer will give to the lender or seller to purchase the property; the balance of the selling price is then considered the mortgage.

E

EARNEST MONEY Usually non-refundable, earnest money is used as a good-faith binder to secure the buyer's intent to purchase the property in question.

EASEMENT Interest in land owned by another individual or company that entitles its holder to a limited use or access to the property for a gas-line easement, for example.

ENCUMBRANCE Easements, liens, or other conditions viewed as undesirable causing property to decrease in value if placed on the title.

EQUITY Value of property (minus the liens) which is built up over time.

ESCROW When money is held as good faith on a property, it is held in escrow meaning it is held by a mutual party with no vested interest in favoring one party over the other.

ESTATE A person's entire holdings, including real estate and other valuables.

EXPENSES All the costs of doing business which can include desk fees, agent fees for advertising, and other factors considered to be expenses for real estate agents.

EXPIRED Past real estate listings in the MLS which did not sell during the designated time allotted for the listing agreement.

F

FEDERAL HOME LOAN MORTGAGE CORPORATION Government agency that buys home mortgages referred to commonly as Freddie Mac.

FEDERAL HOUSING ADMINISTRATION (FHA) Lenders use this federal agency to secure first mortgages covering a large portion of the total real estate price. These loans are commonly assumable.

FEDERAL NATIONAL MORTGAGE ASSOCIATION An agency of the Department of Housing and Urban Development that secures mortgages. Referred to commonly as Fannie Mae.

FINANCING The money a lender is loaning to the borrower for a set number of years with a repayment plan.

FIXED RATE MORTGAGE Many conventional mortgages will offer a fixed rate meaning the rate of interest will remain the same for the term of the loan.

FORECLOSURE A foreclosure occurs when a party initiates force to secure funds due them. A foreclosure occurs when real estate is attached to liens and the borrower cannot pay the mortgage holder or lien holders.

FRANCHISE A nationally recognized business with companies carrying the same company name under the trademark of a franchise organization such as Century21.

FSBO For Sale by Owner

G

GOVERNMENTAL NATIONAL MORTGAGE ASSOCIATION Organization formed by the government that enables the government to help investors collect payments on certain securities. Commonly referred to as Ginnie Mae.

GRADUATED PAYMENT MORTGAGE Mortgage set up with a repayment plan with payments increasing over a period of years until the loan is satisfied.

GRANTEE Usually the buyer in a real estate transaction.

GRANTOR Usually the seller in a real estate transaction.

GROUND LEASE Land being leased to an individual that has absolutely no residential dwelling on the property; or if it does, the ground (or land) is the only portion of the property being leased.

H

HOMEOWNER'S INSURANCE A policy for homeowners that provides protection from theft, fire, and other unforeseen losses.

I

INTEREST ONLY MORTGAGE Loan where the money paid is only interest due until a designated time when the entire loan amount including principal would mature or become due in full.

INTEREST RATE Money charged to the loan amount as the fee for the money's use.

INVESTMENT CLUBS Clubs that concentrate on how to grow and invest money wisely.

J

JUDGMENT A court-ordered lien on a property.

JUNIOR MORTGAGE Mortgage that is second in line behind the first mortgage securing a property.

L

LEASE A contractual agreement that defines the terms of occupancy in a rental situation.

LENDER Generally, the same as a banker; someone who loans money.

LIEN An attachment to a property to secure a loan.

LISTING Indicates that a formal agreement has been signed giving the real estate agent permission to sell the property the listing covers.

LOAN Money made available to an individual with set terms for repayment, usually with an interest rate attached.

LOAN ORIGINATION FEE The fee charged by a lender when a borrower takes out a loan.

M

MARKETABLE TITLE A

deed to a property that has no encumbrances enabling the seller to transfer the property to a buyer and the buyer to buy the property from a seller.

MARKET RENTS The same as a CMA only on rental units; the market rents are rents gained in comparison to other rentals in the same location.

MORTGAGE INSURANCE PREMIUM (MIP) Insurance protecting the lender from loss. Required by FHA.

MORTGAGE A loan used to finance real estate and secured by the property being financed.

MORTGAGEE The lender.

MORTGAGOR The borrower.

MULTIPLE LISTING Service that lists real estate offered for sale by a particular real estate agent that can be shown or sold by other real estate agents within a certain area.

N

NATIONAL ASSOCIATION OF REALTORS The trade association for real estate agents and brokers. Those affiliated with the National Association of Realtors receive the designation of *realtor*.

NET WORTH A person's true worth calculated by taking the person's assets and subtracting his or her debts and liabilities.

O

OPTION A legal agreement that gives exclusive right for a person to buy real estate within a set time that will expire on a given date, when any money paid for the option will be forfeited.

P

PACKAGE MORTGAGE The package mortgage includes personal property and the real estate to secure a note for real estate. A package mortgage is often used for collateral in creative financing for individuals.

PASSIVE INCOME Income gained without any effort from the person receiving the income.

PI Principal and Interest

PITI Principal, Interest, Taxes, and Insurance. The PITI is a term used by agents and lenders.

POINTS One percent of the mortgage.

PRINCIPAL The loan amount before interest and fees are applied.

PROPERTY MANAGER A person who receives a fee for overseeing rental units; a property manager collects rents and oversees the general repairs, maintenance, and leasing of rental units for another person or company.

PRORATING Used commonly in taxes, a proration is a division of expense liability between buyers and sellers.

PURCHASE-MONEY MORTGAGE Mortgage between seller and buyer. Seller provides this type of mortgage to the buyer in seller-financing.

Q

QUALIFICATION The period for a lender to decide if he can extend credit to a buyer. Also called the qualifying period.

R

REAL ESTATE AGENT A person who is licensed to sell and list real estate to make money from the real estate transaction; person licensed to advise others on real estate transactions.

REAL ESTATE BROKER An agent who has met education and requirements to qualify to own their own real estate business and hire other independent agents from whom they will earn a commission of what the agent generates in sales volume.

REAL ESTATE OWNED (REO) Used to describe real estate owned by a lender which is in foreclosure.

REALTOR A designation assigned to a real estate agent who belongs to the real estate trade organization,

The National Association of Realtors.

REFINANCE Process of renewing an old loan usually using the equity within one's current real estate holdings.

RENT-TO-OWN A sales contract which enables a buyer to rent-to-own the property they wish to buy. Typically, a buyer will rent a property until it is paid in full and then the deed transfers from the seller to the buyer.

S

SALES AGREEMENT Known as a contract or sales contract, solid offer to purchase and other terms, this is an agreement between buyer and seller which commits both to a solid real estate transaction. It is usually accompanied by a good faith retainer which is lost should the transaction fall through.

SECONDARY FINANCING Money secured with junior mortgages.

SECONDARY MARKET Describes mortgage market where mortgages are traded.

SECOND MORTGAGE A mortgage attached as a second position behind the first mortgage.

SECTION 8 Government housing program which offers lower-income families the opportunity to rent homes they can afford through private home landlords.

SELLER-FINANCING The process whereby the seller has agreed to finance all or some of the property for the buyer using a first or second mortgage and using a purchase-money mortgage in most cases.

SPLIT FUNDING This occurs when an investor invests in two increments usually through a down payment and a payment at another pre-determined date.

STRATEGIES A system of actions or a game plan for success.

SUCCESS COACH A motivator or speaker who focuses on building a person's self esteem.

SURVEY The map of a

property that shows metes and bounds of the real estate in question. Surveys are commonly requested by lenders when loaning money for farms, commercial property and residential properties with acreage.

T

TARGET The finish line of a goal.

TITLE In real estate, the deed to the property that shows ownership.

TITLE COMPANY A company that handles title searches and often closes a real estate transaction for a real estate attorney.

TITLE INSURANCE Offered by many title companies to guarantee that the property being sold is free of all liens.

TITLE SEARCH A process conducted to check for any liens on the property and to discover the property's rightful owner.

TRANSACTION In real estate, it is the actual real estate deal.

U

UNSECURED LOAN Usually at a much higher rate of interest, the unsecured loan has no collateral attached to guarantee its repayments.

V

VA LOAN Guaranteed by Veterans Administration, a VA loan is for veterans and it is assumable by veterans.

VARIABLE RATE Interest rate which is not at a locked-in rate and will vary based on the prime rate.

W

WARRANTY DEED Issued deed guaranteeing the property is clear of encumbrance.

WHOLESALING Property sold under market value to turn it over quickly for profit.

WRAPAROUND MORTGAGE A mortgage that takes an old mortgage from the seller and covers the new loan of the buyer for the property being sold.

Z

ZONING The use the government allows for a particular piece of real estate. Used to designate residential, commercial, and other permitted uses.

Appendix

Checklists

Home Inspection Checklist for Rental Properties and Handy-
Man Specials

Amortization Chart

Sample Amortized Schedule

Checklist One: Before Closing As the Buyer

_____ Check to be sure all deposits have been credited on the closing statement. If you placed a deposit on the property, ensure it is duly noted on the closing statement.

_____ Be sure the property is free of asbestos, termites, and lead-based paint.

_____ If purchasing a building or shopping center, ensure the property meets all building codes and is not in violation of any city or state codes (or even federal).

_____ Title searches are important and necessary. Before you close on a property, be sure you have a complete title search and take out title insurance.

_____ Watch for easements on the property and find out how they will affect your use of the property.

_____ A final walk-through of any property you buy is highly recommended. You should take pains to check out the appliances and take note of anything amiss since the last time you walked-through the property.

_____ Termite Inspection is a must.

_____ Home Inspection is a must.

_____ Check out the property surrounding the property you are buying. Is there a drainage problem? If so, consider how you can handle this before you buy a property doomed by water problems.

_____ Check gas lines to ensure they are in proper working order.

_____ Gutters and downspouts should be in good condition.

_____ Make sure you understand the legal description of the property and check to ensure it is correct in the final closing documents.

_____ Check out all liens on the property, and if you are not sure all liens are satisfied before you close, you should delay the closing until they are or ensure enough money is placed in an escrow to take care of them after the closing.

_____ Radon is a real problem. Take the time to find out if the property is radon-free.

_____ If the property you are buying is still on a septic tank, take the time to find out everything you can about it such as where the field beds are and when it was pumped last.

_____Know the setbacks of the property lines and be familiar with the property restrictions before you close on a property. Request the restrictions of the property before you close.

Checklist Two: Home Inspection Checklist for Rental Properties and Handy-Man Specials

The following charts are designed for your use when searching for a rental or investment property.

Home Interior	Poor	Average	Excellent
Bedrooms			
Bathrooms			
Floorplan			
Closet Space			
Fireplace/Stove			
Cable/Satellite			
Living Room			
Dining Room			
Den/Study			
Media Room			
Kitchen			
Laundry Room			
Walls and Ceilings			
Carpets and Floors			
Basements/Attics			
Garage			
Bonus/Storage			
Plumbing			
Electrical			
Insulation			
Heating/Cooling			
Paint/Stain			
Sound Barriers			
Overall Interior			

Home's Exterior			
Fencing			
Yard Area			
Gutters			
Roofing			
Patio/Deck			
Screened Porch			
Siding			
Windows			
Landscaping			
General curb appeal			
Garden			
Crawl space			
Foundation			
Driveway			
Sidewalk			
Paint/Stain			
Overall Exterior			

Sample Amortization Tables

The following tables are amortization tables which have been prepared to show you different financing and various repayment methods when creatively financing your real estate purchases. These scenarios are for example purposes only and may not be completely accurate due to other fees in mortgage lending.

Scenario 1

Below, you will find an example of a good seller-financing arrangement. In the example below, the seller agrees to provide financing for the buyer. The investor will buy the home and ask the seller to provide the financing for 60 months. The total of payments will be 61 because the 61st payment is a balloon payment. Remember, in many cases a seller will amortize a payment over the course of 15 to 30 years to help a buyer afford the payment better and then they will expect a large balloon payment at the end. In this case, $60,581.16 is the final payment due on the house.

The breakdown is like this:

- The Principal Amount Borrowed is $100,000.

- There are 12 payments due per year for five years.

- The annual interest rate in this example is 5 percent and it breaks down to a periodic interest rate of 0.4167 percent.

- The Seller wants $1,000 a month as a payment and at the end of 60 months, he will want a final payment of $60,581.16 from the investor/buyer. When all is said and done, the interest paid on the note will be $20,581.16, and the seller will end up with $120,581.16 instead of $100,000 for his home.

Pmt	Principal	Interest	Cm Prin	Cm Int	Prin Bal
1	583.33	416.67	583.33	416.67	99416.67
2	585.76	414.24	1169.09	830.91	98830.91
3	588.20	411.80	1757.29	1242.71	98242.71
4	590.66	409.34	2347.95	1652.05	97652.05
5	593.12	406.88	2941.07	2058.93	97058.93
6	595.59	404.41	3536.66	2463.34	96463.34
7	598.07	401.93	4134.73	2865.27	95865.27
8	600.56	399.44	4735.29	3264.71	95264.71
9	603.06	396.94	5338.35	3661.65	94661.65
10	605.58	394.42	5943.93	4056.07	94056.07
11	608.10	391.90	6552.03	4447.97	93447.97
12	610.63	389.37	7162.66	4837.34	92837.34

Pmt	Principal	Interest	Cm Prin	Cm Int	Prin Bal
13	613.18	386.82	7775.84	5224.16	92224.16
14	615.73	384.27	8391.57	5608.43	91608.43
15	618.30	381.70	9009.87	5990.13	90990.13
16	620.87	379.13	9630.74	6369.26	90369.26
17	623.46	376.54	10254.20	6745.80	89745.80
18	626.06	373.94	10880.26	7119.74	89119.74
19	628.67	371.33	11508.93	7491.07	88491.07
20	631.29	368.71	12140.22	7859.78	87859.78
21	633.92	366.08	12774.14	8225.86	87225.86
22	636.56	363.44	13410.70	8589.30	86589.30
23	639.21	360.79	14049.91	8950.09	85950.09
24	641.87	358.13	14691.78	9308.22	85308.22

Pmt	Principal	Interest	Cm Prin	Cm Int	Prin Bal
25	644.55	355.45	15336.33	9663.67	84663.67
26	647.23	352.77	15983.56	10016.44	84016.44
27	649.93	350.07	16633.49	10366.51	83366.51

28	652.64	347.36	17286.13	10713.87	82713.87
29	655.36	344.64	17941.49	11058.51	82058.51
30	658.09	341.91	18599.58	11400.42	81400.42
31	660.83	339.17	19260.41	11739.59	80739.59
32	663.59	336.41	19924.00	12076.00	80076.00
33	666.35	333.65	20590.35	12409.65	79409.65
34	669.13	330.87	21259.48	12740.52	78740.52
35	671.91	328.09	21931.39	13068.61	78068.61
36	674.71	325.29	22606.10	13393.90	77393.90

37	677.53	322.47	23283.63	13716.37	76716.37
38	680.35	319.65	23963.98	14036.02	76036.02
39	683.18	316.82	24647.16	14352.84	75352.84
40	686.03	313.97	25333.19	14666.81	74666.81
41	688.89	311.11	26022.08	14977.92	73977.92
42	691.76	308.24	26713.84	15286.16	73286.16
43	694.64	305.36	27408.48	15591.52	72591.52
44	697.54	302.46	28106.02	15893.98	71893.98
45	700.44	299.56	28806.46	16193.54	71193.54
46	703.36	296.64	29509.82	16490.18	70490.18
47	706.29	293.71	30216.11	16783.89	69783.89
48	709.23	290.77	30925.34	17074.66	69074.66

49	712.19	287.81	31637.53	17362.47	68362.47
50	715.16	284.84	32352.69	17647.31	67647.31
51	718.14	281.86	33070.83	17929.17	66929.17
52	721.13	278.87	33791.96	18208.04	66208.04
53	724.13	275.87	34516.09	18483.91	65483.91
54	727.15	272.85	35243.24	18756.76	64756.76
55	730.18	269.82	35973.42	19026.58	64026.58
56	733.22	266.78	36706.64	19293.36	63293.36
57	736.28	263.72	37442.92	19557.08	62557.08

58	739.35	260.65	38182.27	19817.73	61817.73
59	742.43	257.57	38924.70	20075.30	61075.30
60	745.52	254.48	39670.22	20329.78	60329.78

| 61 | *60329.78 | 251.37 | 100000.00 | 20581.15 | 0.00 |

The final payment # 61 is the Balloon Payment.

Scenario 2

Below, you will find an example of a lot sold for $12,000 with owner-financing available. The seller is financing the entire $12,000 for the buyer. He wants the buyer to complete his financial obligations within 60 months. The interest rate offered is 8 percent and the payment is $243.32 per month. In this case, at the end of five years, the buyer owns the lot free and clear and the seller makes an additional $2598.97 on his lot with the total amount paid to the seller at $14,598.97

Pmt	Principal	Interest	Cm Prin	Cm Int	Prin Bal
1	163.32	80.00	163.32	80.00	11836.68
2	164.41	78.91	327.73	158.91	11672.27
3	165.50	77.82	493.23	236.73	11506.77
4	166.61	76.71	659.84	313.44	11340.16
5	167.72	75.60	827.56	389.04	11172.44
6	168.84	74.48	996.40	463.52	11003.60
7	169.96	73.36	1166.36	536.88	10833.64
8	171.10	72.22	1337.46	609.10	10662.54
9	172.24	71.08	1509.70	680.18	10490.30
10	173.38	69.94	1683.08	750.12	10316.92
11	174.54	68.78	1857.62	818.90	10142.38
12	175.70	67.62	2033.32	886.52	9966.68

13	176.88	66.44	2210.20	952.96	9789.80
14	178.05	65.27	2388.25	1018.23	9611.75
15	179.24	64.08	2567.49	1082.31	9432.51
16	180.44	62.88	2747.93	1145.19	9252.07
17	181.64	61.68	2929.57	1206.87	9070.43
18	182.85	60.47	3112.42	1267.34	8887.58
19	184.07	59.25	3296.49	1326.59	8703.51
20	185.30	58.02	3481.79	1384.61	8518.21
21	186.53	56.79	3668.32	1441.40	8331.68
22	187.78	55.54	3856.10	1496.94	8143.90
23	189.03	54.29	4045.13	1551.23	7954.87
24	190.29	53.03	4235.42	1604.26	7764.58

25	191.56	51.76	4426.98	1656.02	7573.02
26	192.83	50.49	4619.81	1706.51	7380.19
27	194.12	49.20	4813.93	1755.71	7186.07
28	195.41	47.91	5009.34	1803.62	6990.66
29	196.72	46.60	5206.06	1850.22	6793.94
30	198.03	45.29	5404.09	1895.51	6595.91
31	199.35	43.97	5603.44	1939.48	6396.56
32	200.68	42.64	5804.12	1982.12	6195.88
33	202.01	41.31	6006.13	2023.43	5993.87
34	203.36	39.96	6209.49	2063.39	5790.51
35	204.72	38.60	6414.21	2101.99	5585.79
36	206.08	37.24	6620.29	2139.23	5379.71

37	207.46	35.86	6827.75	2175.09	5172.25
38	208.84	34.48	7036.59	2209.57	4963.41
39	210.23	33.09	7246.82	2242.66	4753.18
40	211.63	31.69	7458.45	2274.35	4541.55
41	213.04	30.28	7671.49	2304.63	4328.51
42	214.46	28.86	7885.95	2333.49	4114.05

43	215.89	27.43	8101.84	2360.92	3898.16
44	217.33	25.99	8319.17	2386.91	3680.83
45	218.78	24.54	8537.95	2411.45	3462.05
46	220.24	23.08	8758.19	2434.53	3241.81
47	221.71	21.61	8979.90	2456.14	3020.10
48	223.19	20.13	9203.09	2476.27	2796.91

49	224.67	18.65	9427.76	2494.92	2572.24
50	226.17	17.15	9653.93	2512.07	2346.07
51	227.68	15.64	9881.61	2527.71	2118.39
52	229.20	14.12	10110.81	2541.83	1889.19
53	230.73	12.59	10341.54	2554.42	1658.46
54	232.26	11.06	10573.80	2565.48	1426.20
55	233.81	9.51	10807.61	2574.99	1192.39
56	235.37	7.95	11042.98	2582.94	957.02
57	236.94	6.38	11279.92	2589.32	720.08
58	238.52	4.80	11518.44	2594.12	481.56
59	240.11	3.21	11758.55	2597.33	241.45
60	241.71	1.61	12000.26	2598.94	-0.26

61	-0.26	0.00	12000.00	2598.94	-0.00

Scenario 3

The following is a typical repayment schedule for $150,000. There are 12 payments per year with the interest rate of 7.5 percent. The payment amount is set at $1048.82. At the end of 30 years, the loan will be paid in full and the bank would have made a total of $227,577.59 in INTEREST alone. The total amount the buyer would have paid for the house will then be $377,577.59.

Pmt	Principal	Interest	Cm Prin	Cm Int	Prin Bal
1	111.32	937.50	111.32	937.50	149888.68
2	112.02	936.80	223.34	1874.30	149776.66
3	112.72	936.10	336.06	2810.40	149663.94
4	113.42	935.40	449.48	3745.80	149550.52
5	114.13	934.69	563.61	4680.49	149436.39
6	114.84	933.98	678.45	5614.47	149321.55
7	115.56	933.26	794.01	6547.73	149205.99
8	116.28	932.54	910.29	7480.27	149089.71
9	117.01	931.81	1027.30	8412.08	148972.70
10	117.74	931.08	1145.04	9343.16	148854.96
11	118.48	930.34	1263.52	10273.50	148736.48
12	119.22	929.60	1382.74	11203.10	148617.26

Pmt	Principal	Interest	Cm Prin	Cm Int	Prin Bal
13	119.96	928.86	1502.70	12131.96	148497.30
14	120.71	928.11	1623.41	13060.07	148376.59
15	121.47	927.35	1744.88	13987.42	148255.12
16	122.23	926.59	1867.11	14914.01	148132.89
17	122.99	925.83	1990.10	15839.84	148009.90
18	123.76	925.06	2113.86	16764.90	147886.14
19	124.53	924.29	2238.39	17689.19	147761.61
20	125.31	923.51	2363.70	18612.70	147636.30
21	126.09	922.73	2489.79	19535.43	147510.21
22	126.88	921.94	2616.67	20457.37	147383.33
23	127.67	921.15	2744.34	21378.52	147255.66
24	128.47	920.35	2872.81	22298.87	147127.19

Pmt	Principal	Interest	Cm Prin	Cm Int	Prin Bal
25	129.28	919.54	3002.09	23218.41	146997.91
26	130.08	918.74	3132.17	24137.15	146867.83
27	130.90	917.92	3263.07	25055.07	146736.93
28	131.71	917.11	3394.78	25972.18	146605.22
29	132.54	916.28	3527.32	26888.46	146472.68

30	133.37	915.45	3660.69	27803.91	146339.31
31	134.20	914.62	3794.89	28718.53	146205.11
32	135.04	913.78	3929.93	29632.31	146070.07
33	135.88	912.94	4065.81	30545.25	145934.19
34	136.73	912.09	4202.54	31457.34	145797.46
35	137.59	911.23	4340.13	32368.57	145659.87
36	138.45	910.37	4478.58	33278.94	145521.42

37	139.31	909.51	4617.89	34188.45	145382.11
38	140.18	908.64	4758.07	35097.09	145241.93
39	141.06	907.76	4899.13	36004.85	145100.87
40	141.94	906.88	5041.07	36911.73	144958.93
41	142.83	905.99	5183.90	37817.72	144816.10
42	143.72	905.10	5327.62	38722.82	144672.38
43	144.62	904.20	5472.24	39627.02	144527.76
44	145.52	903.30	5617.76	40530.32	144382.24
45	146.43	902.39	5764.19	41432.71	144235.81
46	147.35	901.47	5911.54	42334.18	144088.46
47	148.27	900.55	6059.81	43234.73	143940.19
48	149.19	899.63	6209.00	44134.36	143791.00

49	150.13	898.69	6359.13	45033.05	143640.87
50	151.06	897.76	6510.19	45930.81	143489.81
51	152.01	896.81	6662.20	46827.62	143337.80
52	152.96	895.86	6815.16	47723.48	143184.84
53	153.91	894.91	6969.07	48618.39	143030.93
54	154.88	893.94	7123.95	49512.33	142876.05
55	155.84	892.98	7279.79	50405.31	142720.21
56	156.82	892.00	7436.61	51297.31	142563.39
57	157.80	891.02	7594.41	52188.33	142405.59
58	158.79	890.03	7753.20	53078.36	142246.80
59	159.78	889.04	7912.98	53967.40	142087.02

| 60 | 160.78 | 888.04 | 8073.76 | 54855.44 | 141926.24 |

61	161.78	887.04	8235.54	55742.48	141764.46
62	162.79	886.03	8398.33	56628.51	141601.67
63	163.81	885.01	8562.14	57513.52	141437.86
64	164.83	883.99	8726.97	58397.51	141273.03
65	165.86	882.96	8892.83	59280.47	141107.17
66	166.90	881.92	9059.73	60162.39	140940.27
67	167.94	880.88	9227.67	61043.27	140772.33
68	168.99	879.83	9396.66	61923.10	140603.34
69	170.05	878.77	9566.71	62801.87	140433.29
70	171.11	877.71	9737.82	63679.58	140262.18
71	172.18	876.64	9910.00	64556.22	140090.00
72	173.26	875.56	10083.26	65431.78	139916.74

73	174.34	874.48	10257.60	66306.26	139742.40
74	175.43	873.39	10433.03	67179.65	139566.97
75	176.53	872.29	10609.56	68051.94	139390.44
76	177.63	871.19	10787.19	68923.13	139212.81
77	178.74	870.08	10965.93	69793.21	139034.07
78	179.86	868.96	11145.79	70662.17	138854.21
79	180.98	867.84	11326.77	71530.01	138673.23
80	182.11	866.71	11508.88	72396.72	138491.12
81	183.25	865.57	11692.13	73262.29	138307.87
82	184.40	864.42	11876.53	74126.71	138123.47
83	185.55	863.27	12062.08	74989.98	137937.92
84	186.71	862.11	12248.79	75852.09	137751.21

85	187.87	860.95	12436.66	76713.04	137563.34
86	189.05	859.77	12625.71	77572.81	137374.29
87	190.23	858.59	12815.94	78431.40	137184.06
88	191.42	857.40	13007.36	79288.80	136992.64

89	192.62	856.20	13199.98	80145.00	136800.02
90	193.82	855.00	13393.80	81000.00	136606.20
91	195.03	853.79	13588.83	81853.79	136411.17
92	196.25	852.57	13785.08	82706.36	136214.92
93	197.48	851.34	13982.56	83557.70	136017.44
94	198.71	850.11	14181.27	84407.81	135818.73
95	199.95	848.87	14381.22	85256.68	135618.78
96	201.20	847.62	14582.42	86104.30	135417.58

97	202.46	846.36	14784.88	86950.66	135215.12
98	203.73	845.09	14988.61	87795.75	135011.39
99	205.00	843.82	15193.61	88639.57	134806.39
100	206.28	842.54	15399.89	89482.11	134600.11
101	207.57	841.25	15607.46	90323.36	134392.54
102	208.87	839.95	15816.33	91163.31	134183.67
103	210.17	838.65	16026.50	92001.96	133973.50
104	211.49	837.33	16237.99	92839.29	133762.01
105	212.81	836.01	16450.80	93675.30	133549.20
106	214.14	834.68	16664.94	94509.98	133335.06
107	215.48	833.34	16880.42	95343.32	133119.58
108	216.82	832.00	17097.24	96175.32	132902.76

109	218.18	830.64	17315.42	97005.96	132684.58
110	219.54	829.28	17534.96	97835.24	132465.04
111	220.91	827.91	17755.87	98663.15	132244.13
112	222.29	826.53	17978.16	99489.68	132021.84
113	223.68	825.14	18201.84	100314.82	131798.16
114	225.08	823.74	18426.92	101138.56	131573.08
115	226.49	822.33	18653.41	101960.89	131346.59
116	227.90	820.92	18881.31	102781.81	131118.69
117	229.33	819.49	19110.64	103601.30	130889.36
118	230.76	818.06	19341.40	104419.36	130658.60

119	232.20	816.62	19573.60	105235.98	130426.40
120	233.65	815.17	19807.25	106051.15	130192.75

121	235.12	813.70	20042.37	106864.85	129957.63
122	236.58	812.24	20278.95	107677.09	129721.05
123	238.06	810.76	20517.01	108487.85	129482.99
124	239.55	809.27	20756.56	109297.12	129243.44
125	241.05	807.77	20997.61	110104.89	129002.39
126	242.56	806.26	21240.17	110911.15	128759.83
127	244.07	804.75	21484.24	111715.90	128515.76
128	245.60	803.22	21729.84	112519.12	128270.16
129	247.13	801.69	21976.97	113320.81	128023.03
130	248.68	800.14	22225.65	114120.95	127774.35
131	250.23	798.59	22475.88	114919.54	127524.12
132	251.79	797.03	22727.67	115716.57	127272.33

133	253.37	795.45	22981.04	116512.02	127018.96
134	254.95	793.87	23235.99	117305.89	126764.01
135	256.54	792.28	23492.53	118098.17	126507.47
136	258.15	790.67	23750.68	118888.84	126249.32
137	259.76	789.06	24010.44	119677.90	125989.56
138	261.39	787.43	24271.83	120465.33	125728.17
139	263.02	785.80	24534.85	121251.13	125465.15
140	264.66	784.16	24799.51	122035.29	125200.49
141	266.32	782.50	25065.83	122817.79	124934.17
142	267.98	780.84	25333.81	123598.63	124666.19
143	269.66	779.16	25603.47	124377.79	124396.53
144	271.34	777.48	25874.81	125155.27	124125.19

145	273.04	775.78	26147.85	125931.05	123852.15
146	274.74	774.08	26422.59	126705.13	123577.41
147	276.46	772.36	26699.05	127477.49	123300.95

148	278.19	770.63	26977.24	128248.12	123022.76
149	279.93	768.89	27257.17	129017.01	122742.83
150	281.68	767.14	27538.85	129784.15	122461.15
151	283.44	765.38	27822.29	130549.53	122177.71
152	285.21	763.61	28107.50	131313.14	121892.50
153	286.99	761.83	28394.49	132074.97	121605.51
154	288.79	760.03	28683.28	132835.00	121316.72
155	290.59	758.23	28973.87	133593.23	121026.13
156	292.41	756.41	29266.28	134349.64	120733.72

157	294.23	754.59	29560.51	135104.23	120439.49
158	296.07	752.75	29856.58	135856.98	120143.42
159	297.92	750.90	30154.50	136607.88	119845.50
160	299.79	749.03	30454.29	137356.91	119545.71
161	301.66	747.16	30755.95	138104.07	119244.05
162	303.54	745.28	31059.49	138849.35	118940.51
163	305.44	743.38	31364.93	139592.73	118635.07
164	307.35	741.47	31672.28	140334.20	118327.72
165	309.27	739.55	31981.55	141073.75	118018.45
166	311.20	737.62	32292.75	141811.37	117707.25
167	313.15	735.67	32605.90	142547.04	117394.10
168	315.11	733.71	32921.01	143280.75	117078.99

169	317.08	731.74	33238.09	144012.49	116761.91
170	319.06	729.76	33557.15	144742.25	116442.85
171	321.05	727.77	33878.20	145470.02	116121.80
172	323.06	725.76	34201.26	146195.78	115798.74
173	325.08	723.74	34526.34	146919.52	115473.66
174	327.11	721.71	34853.45	147641.23	115146.55
175	329.15	719.67	35182.60	148360.90	114817.40
176	331.21	717.61	35513.81	149078.51	114486.19
177	333.28	715.54	35847.09	149794.05	114152.91

178	335.36	713.46	36182.45	150507.51	113817.55
179	337.46	711.36	36519.91	151218.87	113480.09
180	339.57	709.25	36859.48	151928.12	113140.52

181	341.69	707.13	37201.17	152635.25	112798.83
182	343.83	704.99	37545.00	153340.24	112455.00
183	345.98	702.84	37890.98	154043.08	112109.02
184	348.14	700.68	38239.12	154743.76	111760.88
185	350.31	698.51	38589.43	155442.27	111410.57
186	352.50	696.32	38941.93	156138.59	111058.07
187	354.71	694.11	39296.64	156832.70	110703.36
188	356.92	691.90	39653.56	157524.60	110346.44
189	359.15	689.67	40012.71	158214.27	109987.29
190	361.40	687.42	40374.11	158901.69	109625.89
191	363.66	685.16	40737.77	159586.85	109262.23
192	365.93	682.89	41103.70	160269.74	108896.30

193	368.22	680.60	41471.92	160950.34	108528.08
194	370.52	678.30	41842.44	161628.64	108157.56
195	372.84	675.98	42215.28	162304.62	107784.72
196	375.17	673.65	42590.45	162978.27	107409.55
197	377.51	671.31	42967.96	163649.58	107032.04
198	379.87	668.95	43347.83	164318.53	106652.17
199	382.24	666.58	43730.07	164985.11	106269.93
200	384.63	664.19	44114.70	165649.30	105885.30
201	387.04	661.78	44501.74	166311.08	105498.26
202	389.46	659.36	44891.20	166970.44	105108.80
203	391.89	656.93	45283.09	167627.37	104716.91
204	394.34	654.48	45677.43	168281.85	104322.57

205	396.80	652.02	46074.23	168933.87	103925.77
206	399.28	649.54	46473.51	169583.41	103526.49
207	401.78	647.04	46875.29	170230.45	103124.71

208	404.29	644.53	47279.58	170874.98	102720.42
209	406.82	642.00	47686.40	171516.98	102313.60
210	409.36	639.46	48095.76	172156.44	101904.24
211	411.92	636.90	48507.68	172793.34	101492.32
212	414.49	634.33	48922.17	173427.67	101077.83
213	417.08	631.74	49339.25	174059.41	100660.75
214	419.69	629.13	49758.94	174688.54	100241.06
215	422.31	626.51	50181.25	175315.05	99818.75
216	424.95	623.87	50606.20	175938.92	99393.80

217	427.61	621.21	51033.81	176560.13	98966.19
218	430.28	618.54	51464.09	177178.67	98535.91
219	432.97	615.85	51897.06	177794.52	98102.94
220	435.68	613.14	52332.74	178407.66	97667.26
221	438.40	610.42	52771.14	179018.08	97228.86
222	441.14	607.68	53212.28	179625.76	96787.72
223	443.90	604.92	53656.18	180230.68	96343.82
224	446.67	602.15	54102.85	180832.83	95897.15
225	449.46	599.36	54552.31	181432.19	95447.69
226	452.27	596.55	55004.58	182028.74	94995.42
227	455.10	593.72	55459.68	182622.46	94540.32
228	457.94	590.88	55917.62	183213.34	94082.38

229	460.81	588.01	56378.43	183801.35	93621.57
230	463.69	585.13	56842.12	184386.48	93157.88
231	466.58	582.24	57308.70	184968.72	92691.30
232	469.50	579.32	57778.20	185548.04	92221.80
233	472.43	576.39	58250.63	186124.43	91749.37
234	475.39	573.43	58726.02	186697.86	91273.98
235	478.36	570.46	59204.38	187268.32	90795.62
236	481.35	567.47	59685.73	187835.79	90314.27
237	484.36	564.46	60170.09	188400.25	89829.91

238	487.38	561.44	60657.47	188961.69	89342.53
239	490.43	558.39	61147.90	189520.08	88852.10
240	493.49	555.33	61641.39	190075.41	88358.61

241	496.58	552.24	62137.97	190627.65	87862.03
242	499.68	549.14	62637.65	191176.79	87362.35
243	502.81	546.01	63140.46	191722.80	86859.54
244	505.95	542.87	63646.41	192265.67	86353.59
245	509.11	539.71	64155.52	192805.38	85844.48
246	512.29	536.53	64667.81	193341.91	85332.19
247	515.49	533.33	65183.30	193875.24	84816.70
248	518.72	530.10	65702.02	194405.34	84297.98
249	521.96	526.86	66223.98	194932.20	83776.02
250	525.22	523.60	66749.20	195455.80	83250.80
251	528.50	520.32	67277.70	195976.12	82722.30
252	531.81	517.01	67809.51	196493.13	82190.49

253	535.13	513.69	68344.64	197006.82	81655.36
254	538.47	510.35	68883.11	197517.17	81116.89
255	541.84	506.98	69424.95	198024.15	80575.05
256	545.23	503.59	69970.18	198527.74	80029.82
257	548.63	500.19	70518.81	199027.93	79481.19
258	552.06	496.76	71070.87	199524.69	78929.13
259	555.51	493.31	71626.38	200018.00	78373.62
260	558.98	489.84	72185.36	200507.84	77814.64
261	562.48	486.34	72747.84	200994.18	77252.16
262	565.99	482.83	73313.83	201477.01	76686.17
263	569.53	479.29	73883.36	201956.30	76116.64
264	573.09	475.73	74456.45	202432.03	75543.55

265	576.67	472.15	75033.12	202904.18	74966.88
266	580.28	468.54	75613.40	203372.72	74386.60

267	583.90	464.92	76197.30	203837.64	73802.70
268	587.55	461.27	76784.85	204298.91	73215.15
269	591.23	457.59	77376.08	204756.50	72623.92
270	594.92	453.90	77971.00	205210.40	72029.00
271	598.64	450.18	78569.64	205660.58	71430.36
272	602.38	446.44	79172.02	206107.02	70827.98
273	606.15	442.67	79778.17	206549.69	70221.83
274	609.93	438.89	80388.10	206988.58	69611.90
275	613.75	435.07	81001.85	207423.65	68998.15
276	617.58	431.24	81619.43	207854.89	68380.57

277	621.44	427.38	82240.87	208282.27	67759.13
278	625.33	423.49	82866.20	208705.76	67133.80
279	629.23	419.59	83495.43	209125.35	66504.57
280	633.17	415.65	84128.60	209541.00	65871.40
281	637.12	411.70	84765.72	209952.70	65234.28
282	641.11	407.71	85406.83	210360.41	64593.17
283	645.11	403.71	86051.94	210764.12	63948.06
284	649.14	399.68	86701.08	211163.80	63298.92
285	653.20	395.62	87354.28	211559.42	62645.72
286	657.28	391.54	88011.56	211950.96	61988.44
287	661.39	387.43	88672.95	212338.39	61327.05
288	665.53	383.29	89338.48	212721.68	60661.52

289	669.69	379.13	90008.17	213100.81	59991.83
290	673.87	374.95	90682.04	213475.76	59317.96
291	678.08	370.74	91360.12	213846.50	58639.88
292	682.32	366.50	92042.44	214213.00	57957.56
293	686.59	362.23	92729.03	214575.23	57270.97
294	690.88	357.94	93419.91	214933.17	56580.09
295	695.19	353.63	94115.10	215286.80	55884.90
296	699.54	349.28	94814.64	215636.08	55185.36

297	703.91	344.91	95518.55	215980.99	54481.45
298	708.31	340.51	96226.86	216321.50	53773.14
299	712.74	336.08	96939.60	216657.58	53060.40
300	717.19	331.63	97656.79	216989.21	52343.21

301	721.67	327.15	98378.46	217316.36	51621.54
302	726.19	322.63	99104.65	217638.99	50895.35
303	730.72	318.10	99835.37	217957.09	50164.63
304	735.29	313.53	100570.66	218270.62	49429.34
305	739.89	308.93	101310.55	218579.55	48689.45
306	744.51	304.31	102055.06	218883.86	47944.94
307	749.16	299.66	102804.22	219183.52	47195.78
308	753.85	294.97	103558.07	219478.49	46441.93
309	758.56	290.26	104316.63	219768.75	45683.37
310	763.30	285.52	105079.93	220054.27	44920.07
311	768.07	280.75	105848.00	220335.02	44152.00
312	772.87	275.95	106620.87	220610.97	43379.13

313	777.70	271.12	107398.57	220882.09	42601.43
314	782.56	266.26	108181.13	221148.35	41818.87
315	787.45	261.37	108968.58	221409.72	41031.42
316	792.37	256.45	109760.95	221666.17	40239.05
317	797.33	251.49	110558.28	221917.66	39441.72
318	802.31	246.51	111360.59	222164.17	38639.41
319	807.32	241.50	112167.91	222405.67	37832.09
320	812.37	236.45	112980.28	222642.12	37019.72
321	817.45	231.37	113797.73	222873.49	36202.27
322	822.56	226.26	114620.29	223099.75	35379.71
323	827.70	221.12	115447.99	223320.87	34552.01
324	832.87	215.95	116280.86	223536.82	33719.14

| 325 | 838.08 | 210.74 | 117118.94 | 223747.56 | 32881.06 |
| 326 | 843.31 | 205.51 | 117962.25 | 223953.07 | 32037.75 |

327	848.58	200.24	118810.83	224153.31	31189.17
328	853.89	194.93	119664.72	224348.24	30335.28
329	859.22	189.60	120523.94	224537.84	29476.06
330	864.59	184.23	121388.53	224722.07	28611.47
331	870.00	178.82	122258.53	224900.89	27741.47
332	875.44	173.38	123133.97	225074.27	26866.03
333	880.91	167.91	124014.88	225242.18	25985.12
334	886.41	162.41	124901.29	225404.59	25098.71
335	891.95	156.87	125793.24	225561.46	24206.76
336	897.53	151.29	126690.77	225712.75	23309.23

337	903.14	145.68	127593.91	225858.43	22406.09
338	908.78	140.04	128502.69	225998.47	21497.31
339	914.46	134.36	129417.15	226132.83	20582.85
340	920.18	128.64	130337.33	226261.47	19662.67
341	925.93	122.89	131263.26	226384.36	18736.74
342	931.72	117.10	132194.98	226501.46	17805.02
343	937.54	111.28	133132.52	226612.74	16867.48
344	943.40	105.42	134075.92	226718.16	15924.08
345	949.29	99.53	135025.21	226817.69	14974.79
346	955.23	93.59	135980.44	226911.28	14019.56
347	961.20	87.62	136941.64	226998.90	13058.36
348	967.21	81.61	137908.85	227080.51	12091.15

349	973.25	75.57	138882.10	227156.08	11117.90
350	979.33	69.49	139861.43	227225.57	10138.57
351	985.45	63.37	140846.88	227288.94	9153.12
352	991.61	57.21	141838.49	227346.15	8161.51
353	997.81	51.01	142836.30	227397.16	7163.70
354	1004.05	44.77	143840.35	227441.93	6159.65
355	1010.32	38.50	144850.67	227480.43	5149.33
356	1016.64	32.18	145867.31	227512.61	4132.69
357	1022.99	25.83	146890.30	227538.44	3109.70

358	1029.38	19.44	147919.68	227557.88	2080.32
359	1035.82	13.00	148955.50	227570.88	1044.50
360	1042.29	6.53	149997.79	227577.41	2.21

| 361 | *2.21 | 0.01 | 150000.00 | 227577.42 | -0.00 |

Scenario 4

The following scenario is for a larger home that sells for $275,000. The total number of payments is 121 with an interest rate of 5 percent. The mortgage payment each month to be paid to the seller is $2,200 and the final payment will be at the balloon payment amount of $111,770.37. So after 10 years, the home buyer will still need to finance the remaining balloon payment or plan on winning a lottery.

In this scenario, we see why seller-financing is lucrative. The seller financed his $275,000 home to the buyer. During the course of 10 years, he earned $100,770.37 in interest. He will make a total of $375,770.37 on a home he planned on selling for only $275,000.

Pmt	Principal	Interest	Cm Prin	Cm Int	Prin Bal
1	1054.17	1145.83	1054.17	1145.83	273945.83
2	1058.56	1141.44	2112.73	2287.27	272887.27
3	1062.97	1137.03	3175.70	3424.30	271824.30
4	1067.40	1132.60	4243.10	4556.90	270756.90
5	1071.85	1128.15	5314.95	5685.05	269685.05
6	1076.31	1123.69	6391.26	6808.74	268608.74
7	1080.80	1119.20	7472.06	7927.94	267527.94
8	1085.30	1114.70	8557.36	9042.64	266442.64
9	1089.82	1110.18	9647.18	10152.82	265352.82
10	1094.36	1105.64	10741.54	11258.46	264258.46

11	1098.92	1101.08	11840.46	12359.54	263159.54
12	1103.50	1096.50	12943.96	13456.04	262056.04

13	1108.10	1091.90	14052.06	14547.94	260947.94
14	1112.72	1087.28	15164.78	15635.22	259835.22
15	1117.35	1082.65	16282.13	16717.87	258717.87
16	1122.01	1077.99	17404.14	17795.86	257595.86
17	1126.68	1073.32	18530.82	18869.18	256469.18
18	1131.38	1068.62	19662.20	19937.80	255337.80
19	1136.09	1063.91	20798.29	21001.71	254201.71
20	1140.83	1059.17	21939.12	22060.88	253060.88
21	1145.58	1054.42	23084.70	23115.30	251915.30
22	1150.35	1049.65	24235.05	24164.95	250764.95
23	1155.15	1044.85	25390.20	25209.80	249609.80
24	1159.96	1040.04	26550.16	26249.84	248449.84

25	1164.79	1035.21	27714.95	27285.05	247285.05
26	1169.65	1030.35	28884.60	28315.40	246115.40
27	1174.52	1025.48	30059.12	29340.88	244940.88
28	1179.41	1020.59	31238.53	30361.47	243761.47
29	1184.33	1015.67	32422.86	31377.14	242577.14
30	1189.26	1010.74	33612.12	32387.88	241387.88
31	1194.22	1005.78	34806.34	33393.66	240193.66
32	1199.19	1000.81	36005.53	34394.47	238994.47
33	1204.19	995.81	37209.72	35390.28	237790.28
34	1209.21	990.79	38418.93	36381.07	236581.07
35	1214.25	985.75	39633.18	37366.82	235366.82
36	1219.30	980.70	40852.48	38347.52	234147.52

37	1224.39	975.61	42076.87	39323.13	232923.13
38	1229.49	970.51	43306.36	40293.64	231693.64
39	1234.61	965.39	44540.97	41259.03	230459.03

40	1239.75	960.25	45780.72	42219.28	229219.28
41	1244.92	955.08	47025.64	43174.36	227974.36
42	1250.11	949.89	48275.75	44124.25	226724.25
43	1255.32	944.68	49531.07	45068.93	225468.93
44	1260.55	939.45	50791.62	46008.38	224208.38
45	1265.80	934.20	52057.42	46942.58	222942.58
46	1271.07	928.93	53328.49	47871.51	221671.51
47	1276.37	923.63	54604.86	48795.14	220395.14
48	1281.69	918.31	55886.55	49713.45	219113.45

49	1287.03	912.97	57173.58	50626.42	217826.42
50	1292.39	907.61	58465.97	51534.03	216534.03
51	1297.77	902.23	59763.74	52436.26	215236.26
52	1303.18	896.82	61066.92	53333.08	213933.08
53	1308.61	891.39	62375.53	54224.47	212624.47
54	1314.06	885.94	63689.59	55110.41	211310.41
55	1319.54	880.46	65009.13	55990.87	209990.87
56	1325.04	874.96	66334.17	56865.83	208665.83
57	1330.56	869.44	67664.73	57735.27	207335.27
58	1336.10	863.90	69000.83	58599.17	205999.17
59	1341.67	858.33	70342.50	59457.50	204657.50
60	1347.26	852.74	71689.76	60310.24	203310.24

61	1352.87	847.13	73042.63	61157.37	201957.37
62	1358.51	841.49	74401.14	61998.86	200598.86
63	1364.17	835.83	75765.31	62834.69	199234.69
64	1369.86	830.14	77135.17	63664.83	197864.83
65	1375.56	824.44	78510.73	64489.27	196489.27
66	1381.29	818.71	79892.02	65307.98	195107.98
67	1387.05	812.95	81279.07	66120.93	193720.93
68	1392.83	807.17	82671.90	66928.10	192328.10
69	1398.63	801.37	84070.53	67729.47	190929.47

70	1404.46	795.54	85474.99	68525.01	189525.01
71	1410.31	789.69	86885.30	69314.70	188114.70
72	1416.19	783.81	88301.49	70098.51	186698.51

73	1422.09	777.91	89723.58	70876.42	185276.42
74	1428.01	771.99	91151.59	71648.41	183848.41
75	1433.96	766.04	92585.55	72414.45	182414.45
76	1439.94	760.06	94025.49	73174.51	180974.51
77	1445.94	754.06	95471.43	73928.57	179528.57
78	1451.96	748.04	96923.39	74676.61	178076.61
79	1458.01	741.99	98381.40	75418.60	176618.60
80	1464.09	735.91	99845.49	76154.51	175154.51
81	1470.19	729.81	101315.68	76884.32	173684.32
82	1476.32	723.68	102792.00	77608.00	172208.00
83	1482.47	717.53	104274.47	78325.53	170725.53
84	1488.64	711.36	105763.11	79036.89	169236.89

85	1494.85	705.15	107257.96	79742.04	167742.04
86	1501.07	698.93	108759.03	80440.97	166240.97
87	1507.33	692.67	110266.36	81133.64	164733.64
88	1513.61	686.39	111779.97	81820.03	163220.03
89	1519.92	680.08	113299.89	82500.11	161700.11
90	1526.25	673.75	114826.14	83173.86	160173.86
91	1532.61	667.39	116358.75	83841.25	158641.25
92	1538.99	661.01	117897.74	84502.26	157102.26
93	1545.41	654.59	119443.15	85156.85	155556.85
94	1551.85	648.15	120995.00	85805.00	154005.00
95	1558.31	641.69	122553.31	86446.69	152446.69
96	1564.81	635.19	124118.12	87081.88	150881.88

97	1571.33	628.67	125689.45	87710.55	149310.55
98	1577.87	622.13	127267.32	88332.68	147732.68

99	1584.45	615.55	128851.77	88948.23	146148.23
100	1591.05	608.95	130442.82	89557.18	144557.18
101	1597.68	602.32	132040.50	90159.50	142959.50
102	1604.34	595.66	133644.84	90755.16	141355.16
103	1611.02	588.98	135255.86	91344.14	139744.14
104	1617.73	582.27	136873.59	91926.41	138126.41
105	1624.47	575.53	138498.06	92501.94	136501.94
106	1631.24	568.76	140129.30	93070.70	134870.70
107	1638.04	561.96	141767.34	93632.66	133232.66
108	1644.86	555.14	143412.20	94187.80	131587.80

109	1651.72	548.28	145063.92	94736.08	129936.08
110	1658.60	541.40	146722.52	95277.48	128277.48
111	1665.51	534.49	148388.03	95811.97	126611.97
112	1672.45	527.55	150060.48	96339.52	124939.52
113	1679.42	520.58	151739.90	96860.10	123260.10
114	1686.42	513.58	153426.32	97373.68	121573.68
115	1693.44	506.56	155119.76	97880.24	119880.24
116	1700.50	499.50	156820.26	98379.74	118179.74
117	1707.58	492.42	158527.84	98872.16	116472.16
118	1714.70	485.30	160242.54	99357.46	114757.46
119	1721.84	478.16	161964.38	99835.62	113035.62
120	1729.02	470.98	163693.40	100306.60	111306.60

| 121 | *111306.60 | 463.78 | 275000.00 | 100770.38 | -0.00 |

Scenario 5

In the following scenario, the buyer of a property needed the seller to help with the down payment and closing costs. The seller agreed to take back a second mortgage and carry the $10,000 used for down payment and closing cost for seven years. In this situation, the buyer will owe the seller $166.01 per month for seven years. The seller sold his home for the purchase price and still ended up making $3,945.06 in interest over a period of seven years.

Pmt	Principal	Interest	Cm Prin	Cm Int	Prin Bal
1	82.68	83.33	82.68	83.33	9917.32
2	83.37	82.64	166.05	165.97	9833.95
3	84.06	81.95	250.11	247.92	9749.89
4	84.76	81.25	334.87	329.17	9665.13
5	85.47	80.54	420.34	409.71	9579.66
6	86.18	79.83	506.52	489.54	9493.48
7	86.90	79.11	593.42	568.65	9406.58
8	87.62	78.39	681.04	647.04	9318.96
9	88.35	77.66	769.39	724.70	9230.61
10	89.09	76.92	858.48	801.62	9141.52
11	89.83	76.18	948.31	877.80	9051.69
12	90.58	75.43	1038.89	953.23	8961.11

Pmt	Principal	Interest	Cm Prin	Cm Int	Prin Bal
13	91.33	74.68	1130.22	1027.91	8869.78
14	92.10	73.91	1222.32	1101.82	8777.68
15	92.86	73.15	1315.18	1174.97	8684.82
16	93.64	72.37	1408.82	1247.34	8591.18
17	94.42	71.59	1503.24	1318.93	8496.76
18	95.20	70.81	1598.44	1389.74	8401.56
19	96.00	70.01	1694.44	1459.75	8305.56
20	96.80	69.21	1791.24	1528.96	8208.76
21	97.60	68.41	1888.84	1597.37	8111.16
22	98.42	67.59	1987.26	1664.96	8012.74
23	99.24	66.77	2086.50	1731.73	7913.50
24	100.06	65.95	2186.56	1797.68	7813.44

Pmt	Principal	Interest	Cm Prin	Cm Int	Prin Bal
25	100.90	65.11	2287.46	1862.79	7712.54
26	101.74	64.27	2389.20	1927.06	7610.80

27	102.59	63.42	2491.79	1990.48	7508.21
28	103.44	62.57	2595.23	2053.05	7404.77
29	104.30	61.71	2699.53	2114.76	7300.47
30	105.17	60.84	2804.70	2175.60	7195.30
31	106.05	59.96	2910.75	2235.56	7089.25
32	106.93	59.08	3017.68	2294.64	6982.32
33	107.82	58.19	3125.50	2352.83	6874.50
34	108.72	57.29	3234.22	2410.12	6765.78
35	109.63	56.38	3343.85	2466.50	6656.15
36	110.54	55.47	3454.39	2521.97	6545.61

37	111.46	54.55	3565.85	2576.52	6434.15
38	112.39	53.62	3678.24	2630.14	6321.76
39	113.33	52.68	3791.57	2682.82	6208.43
40	114.27	51.74	3905.84	2734.56	6094.16
41	115.23	50.78	4021.07	2785.34	5978.93
42	116.19	49.82	4137.26	2835.16	5862.74
43	117.15	48.86	4254.41	2884.02	5745.59
44	118.13	47.88	4372.54	2931.90	5627.46
45	119.11	46.90	4491.65	2978.80	5508.35
46	120.11	45.90	4611.76	3024.70	5388.24
47	121.11	44.90	4732.87	3069.60	5267.13
48	122.12	43.89	4854.99	3113.49	5145.01

49	123.13	42.88	4978.12	3156.37	5021.88
50	124.16	41.85	5102.28	3198.22	4897.72
51	125.20	40.81	5227.48	3239.03	4772.52
52	126.24	39.77	5353.72	3278.80	4646.28
53	127.29	38.72	5481.01	3317.52	4518.99
54	128.35	37.66	5609.36	3355.18	4390.64
55	129.42	36.59	5738.78	3391.77	4261.22
56	130.50	35.51	5869.28	3427.28	4130.72

57	131.59	34.42	6000.87	3461.70	3999.13
58	132.68	33.33	6133.55	3495.03	3866.45
59	133.79	32.22	6267.34	3527.25	3732.66
60	134.90	31.11	6402.24	3558.36	3597.76

61	136.03	29.98	6538.27	3588.34	3461.73
62	137.16	28.85	6675.43	3617.19	3324.57
63	138.31	27.70	6813.74	3644.89	3186.26
64	139.46	26.55	6953.20	3671.44	3046.80
65	140.62	25.39	7093.82	3696.83	2906.18
66	141.79	24.22	7235.61	3721.05	2764.39
67	142.97	23.04	7378.58	3744.09	2621.42
68	144.16	21.85	7522.74	3765.94	2477.26
69	145.37	20.64	7668.11	3786.58	2331.89
70	146.58	19.43	7814.69	3806.01	2185.31
71	147.80	18.21	7962.49	3824.22	2037.51
72	149.03	16.98	8111.52	3841.20	1888.48

73	150.27	15.74	8261.79	3856.94	1738.21
74	151.52	14.49	8413.31	3871.43	1586.69
75	152.79	13.22	8566.10	3884.65	1433.90
76	154.06	11.95	8720.16	3896.60	1279.84
77	155.34	10.67	8875.50	3907.27	1124.50
78	156.64	9.37	9032.14	3916.64	967.86
79	157.94	8.07	9190.08	3924.71	809.92
80	159.26	6.75	9349.34	3931.46	650.66
81	160.59	5.42	9509.93	3936.88	490.07
82	161.93	4.08	9671.86	3940.96	328.14
83	163.28	2.73	9835.14	3943.69	164.86
84	164.64	1.37	9999.78	3945.06	0.22

85	*0.22	0.00	10000.00	3945.06	0.00

References

1. Gallinelli, Frank, *What Every Real Estate Investor Needs to Know About Cash Flow and 36 Other Financial Measures*, McGraw-Hill, 2004. ISBN 0-07-142257-9

2. Cummings, Jack, *Real Estate Finance and Investment Manual*, Prentice Hall, 1997. ISBN 0-13-493388-5

3. Gallinelli, Frank, *Insider Secrets to Financing Your Real Estate Investments*, McGraw-Hill, 2005. ISBN 0-07-144543-9

4. Eldred, Gary, (PHD) The Beginner's Guide to Real Estate Investing, John Wiley and Sons, 2004. ISBN 0-471-64711-X

5. **Forbes.com**

6. **http://en.wikipedia.org/wiki/Contrarian**

7. Navarro, Peter, *If It's Raining in Brazil Buy Starbucks*, McGraw-Hill, 2002. ISBN 0-07-141611-0

8. Conti, Peter and Finkel, David, *Making Big Money Investing in Foreclosures Without Cash or Credit*, Dearborn Financial Publishing, 2003. ISBN 0-7931-7365-5

9. De Roos, Dolf and Burns, Gene, *52 Homes in 52 Weeks*, John Wiley and Sons, Inc., 2006. HD1382.5D4, ISBN-13:978-0-471-75705-4

Author Dedication and Biography

This book is dedicated to my children, Matthew and Amber—
two of the best people I know!

Susan Alvis is the author of four Atlantic Publishing titles including *How to Buy Real Estate Without a Down Payment in any Market*, *The Complete Guide to Purchasing a Condo, Townhouse, or*

Apartment, and *How to Become a Million Dollar Real Estate Agent in Your First Year.* She practiced real estate as a licensed real estate agent in the 1990s and has since placed her license in retirement. Susan writes non-fiction as well as fiction and has several upcoming releases. You can visit her on her Web site at **www.susanalvis.com**. She writes gambling related material and has written for online and offline publications including the print edition of Gambling Online Magazine and others. Susan lives in Northeast Tennessee with her husband Brent and their two children, Matthew and Amber.

Index

Optimize Your REAL ESTATE & INVESTING

HOW TO BUY REAL ESTATE WITHOUT A DOWN PAYMENT IN ANY MARKET: INSIDER SECRETS FROM THE EXPERTS WHO DO IT EVERY DAY

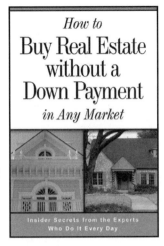

Whether you are a first-time homeowner or an experienced property investor, this is a tremendous guide for buying real estate with no down payment in any market. You will learn the simple formula that can build massive wealth through a real estate purchase with no money down. This proven formula works even if you have no real estate experience, bad or no credit, or very little money. 288 pages.

Item # BRN-02 $21.95

FAST REAL ESTATE PROFITS IN ANY MARKET: THE ART OF FLIPPING PROPERTIES—INSIDER SECRETS FROM THE EXPERTS WHO DO IT EVERY DAY

Real estate flipping refers to the practice of finding a property that is for sale—usually priced below-market—and then selling it soon after it is bought for a quick profit. Finally there's a comprehensive, no-nonsense book that teaches you everything you need to build wealth through flipping properties quickly, legally, and ethically. 288 pages.

Item # FRP-02 $21.95

RETIRE RICH WITH YOUR SELF-DIRECTED IRA: WHAT YOUR BROKER & BANKER DON'T WANT YOU TO KNOW ABOUT MANAGING YOUR OWN RETIREMENT INVESTMENTS

This new book will teach you how to turn your IRA into a wealth-building tool that you control 100%! Take control of your investment future, and make sure your investments are performing for YOU! 392 pages.

Item # RRI-02 $21.95

To order call toll-free 800-814-1132 or visit www.atlantic-pub.com

More **REAL ESTATE & INVESTING** Titles

THE FIRST-TIME HOMEOWNER'S HANDBOOK: A COMPLETE GUIDE AND WORKBOOK FOR THE FIRST-TIME HOME BUYER: WITH COMPANION CD-ROM

In this new book you will find vital information, insight from experts, and great strategies that will allow you to find your dream home faster and feel confident about the purchase. You will learn to avoid some of the most prevalent—and potentially dangerous and expensive—mistakes made by first-time home buyers. 288 pages.

Item # FTH-02 $21.95

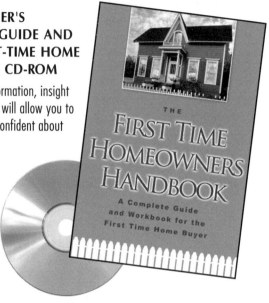

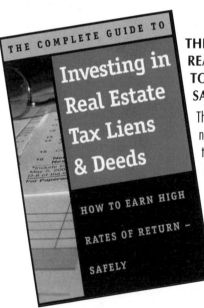

THE COMPLETE GUIDE TO INVESTING IN REAL ESTATE TAX LIENS & DEEDS: HOW TO EARN HIGH RATES OF RETURN—SAFELY

This groundbreaking and exhaustively researched new book will provide everything you need to know to get you started on generating high investment returns with low risk from start to finish. If you are interested in learning hundreds of hints, tricks, and secrets on how to purchase tax liens and deeds and earn enormous profits, then this book is for you. 320 pages.   **Item # CGI-02 $21.95**

To order call toll-free 800-814-1132
or visit www.atlantic-pub.com

Great Titles for SMALL BUSINESS

HOW TO WRITE A GREAT BUSINESS PLAN FOR YOUR SMALL BUSINESS IN 60 MINUTES OR LESS: WITH COMPANION CD-ROM

The importance of a comprehensive, thoughtful business plan cannot be overemphasized. Much hinges on it: outside funding; credit from suppliers; management of your operation and finances; promotion and marketing of your business; achievement of your goals and objectives, yet many small businesses never take the time to prepare one. Now it's easy—and you can do it in less than an hour. This new book and companion CD-ROM will demonstrate how to construct a current and pro-forma balance sheet, an income statement, and a cash flow analysis. You will learn to allocate resources properly, handle unforeseen complications, and make good business decisions. The CD-ROM file (written in Microsoft Word) allows you to simply plug in your own information while providing specific and organized information about your company and how you will repay borrowed money; additionally, it informs sales personnel, suppliers, and others about your operations and goals. 288 pages. **Item # GBP-01 $39.95**

2,001 INNOVATIVE WAYS TO SAVE YOUR COMPANY THOUSANDS BY REDUCING COSTS: A COMPLETE GUIDE TO CREATIVE COST CUTTING AND BOOSTING PROFIT

This new book is full of practical advice on thousands of innovative ways to cut costs in every area of your business. Not only is the idea presented, but the pertinent information is provided for action, such as contact information and Web sites for companies, products, or services recommended. We spent thousands of hours interviewing, e-mailing, and communicating with hundreds of today's most successful small business managers and owners. This book is a compilation of their secrets and proven successful ideas. 288 pages. **Item # IWS-02 $21.95**

THE FRANCHISE HANDBOOK: A COMPLETE GUIDE TO ALL ASPECTS OF BUYING, SELLING OR INVESTING IN A FRANCHISE

According to the U.S. Department of Commerce, buying a franchise is the average person's most viable avenue to owning a business. As a successful small business owner, franchising your existing business plan to others is perhaps your fastest way to growth and enormous profits. This book will be a great resource for both prospective franchisees and franchisors as it explains in detail what the franchise system entails and the precise benefits it offers to both parties.

You will learn franchising advantages and disadvantages, how to develop or purchase a winning concept, how to choose a business franchise that fits your personal style and financial goals, how to develop forecasts and budgets, and how to estimate startup costs. The book also covers managing daily operations, attracting and keeping customers, hiring employees and training staff, securing financing, legal agreements, offerings, markets, real estate, cost control, marketing, international franchising, as well as federal and state franchise regulations. Ensure friendly franchisor/franchisee relationships and build a fortune franchising your own business concept. 288 pages. **Item # TFH-01 $39.95**

To order call toll-free 800-814-1132
or visit www.atlantic-pub.com

Get the most from your EMPLOYEES

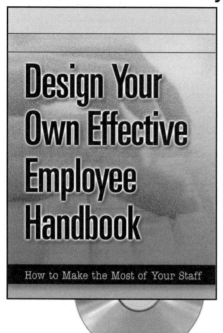

DESIGN YOUR OWN EFFECTIVE EMPLOYEE HANDBOOK: HOW TO MAKE THE MOST OF YOUR STAFF: WITH COMPANION CD-ROM

Our Employee Handbook Template is the ideal solution to produce your own handbook in less than an hour. The companion CD-ROM in MS Word contains the template that you can easily edit for our own purposes; essentially fill in the blank. The book discusses various options you may have in developing the policies. Our employee handbook has been edited and approved by lawyers specializing in employment law. Developing your own handbook now couldn't be easier or less expensive! 288 pages.

Item # GEH-02 $39.95

365 ANSWERS ABOUT HUMAN RESOURCES FOR THE SMALL BUSINESS OWNER: WHAT EVERY MANAGER NEEDS TO KNOW ABOUT WORKPLACE LAW

Finally there is a complete and up-to-date resource for the small business owner. Tired of high legal and consulting fees? This new book is your answer. Detailed are over 300 common questions employers have about employees and the law; it's like having an employment attorney on your staff. Topics include: equal employment opportunity, age discrimination, Americans with Disabilities Act (ADA), unacceptable job performance, termination, substance abuse, drug and alcohol testing, safety, harassment, compensation policies, job classifications, recordkeeping, overtime, employee performance evaluations, wage and salary reviews, payroll, and much more. 288 pages.

Item # HRM-02 $21.95

To order call toll-free 800-814-1132 or visit www.atlantic-pub.com

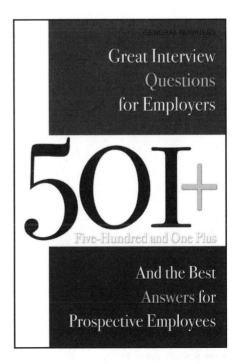

Learn to take advantage of the INTERNET

ONLINE MARKETING SUCCESS STORIES: INSIDER SECRETS FROM THE EXPERTS WHO ARE MAKING MILLIONS ON THE INTERNET TODAY

Standing out in the turmoil of today's Internet marketplace is a major challenge. There are many books and courses on Internet marketing, but this is the only book that will provide you with insider secrets because we asked the marketing experts who make their living on the Internet every day—and they talked. *Online Marketing Success Stories* will give you real-life examples of how successful businesses market their products online. The information is so useful that you can read a page and put the idea into action—today! Learn the most efficient ways to bring consumers to your site, get visitors to purchase, how to up-sell, oversights to avoid, and how to steer clear of years of disappointment. 288 pages. **Item # OMS-02 $21.95**

EBAY INCOME: HOW ANYONE OF ANY AGE, LOCATION AND/OR BACKGROUND CAN BUILD A HIGHLY PROFITABLE ONLINE BUSINESS WITH EBAY

Start making money on eBay today. The book starts with a complete overview of how eBay works. Then the book will guide you through the whole process of creating the auction and auction strategies, photography, writing copy, text and formatting, managing auctions, shipping, collecting payments, registering, About Me page, sources for merchandise, multiple sales, programming tricks, PayPal, accounting, creating marketing, merchandising, managing e-mail lists, advertising plans, taxes and sales tax, best time to list items and for how long, sniping programs, international customers, opening a storefront, electronic commerce, buy-it now pricing, keywords, Google marketing, and eBay secrets; everything you will ever need to get started making money on eBay. 288 pages. **Item # EBY-01 $24.95**

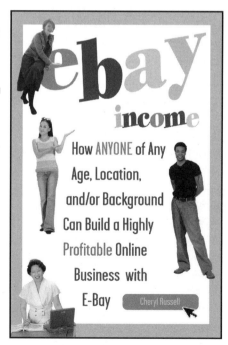

To order call toll-free 800-814-1132 or visit www.atlantic-pub.com

Learn to take advantage of the **INTERNET**

HOW TO USE THE INTERNET TO ADVERTISE, PROMOTE AND MARKET YOUR BUSINESS OR WEB SITE WITH LITTLE OR NO MONEY

Interested in promoting your business and/or Web site, but don't have the big budget for traditional advertising? This new book will show you how to build, promote, and make money off of your Web site or brick and mortar store using the Internet, with minimal costs. Let us arm you with the knowledge you need to make your business a success! Learn how to generate more traffic for your site or store with hundreds of Internet marketing methods, including many free and low-cost promotions. This new book presents a comprehensive, hands-on, step-by-step guide for increasing Web site traffic and traditional store traffic by using hundreds of proven tips, tools, and techniques. 288 pages. **Item # HIA-01 $24.95**

THE EBAY SUCCESS CHRONICLES: SECRETS AND TECHNIQUES EBAY POWERSELLERS USE EVERY DAY TO MAKE MILLIONS

There are many books on eBay, but this is the only one that will provide you with insider secrets because we asked the PowerSeller experts who make their living on eBay every day—and they talked. We spent thousands of hours interviewing and e-mailing eBay PowerSellers. This book is a compilation of their secrets and proven successful ideas. If you are interested in learning hundreds of hints, tricks, and secrets on how to make money (or more money) on eBay, then this book is for you. Currently with over 430,000 sellers make a living off eBay, there is no reason you shouldn't become financially successful. This book will arm you with the knowledge to become an eBay PowerSeller. 288 pages.

Item # ESC-02 $21.95

To order call toll-free **800-814-1132** or visit **www.atlantic-pub.com**

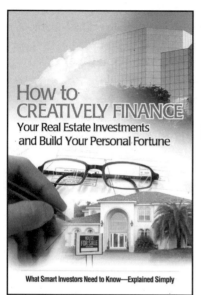

How to
CREATIVELY FINANCE
Your Real Estate Investments
and Build Your Personal Fortune

What Smart Investors Need to Know—Explained Simply

DID YOU BORROW THIS COPY?

Have you been borrowing a copy of *How to Creatively Finance Your Real Estate Investments and Build Your Personal Fortune* from a friend, colleague or library? Wouldn't you like your own copy for quick and easy reference? To order, photocopy the form below and send to:

Atlantic Publishing Company
1405 SW 6th Ave.
Ocala, FL 34474-7014